"Sam Bennett is a genius — really. She has the unique ability to help artists of all types love who they are and love the work they do, and then, get this, she helps them actually get their creative work out into the world in a bigger, better way. *Get It Done* is the book you will come back to time and time again for inspiration, profound truths, humor, and one-of-a-kind practical tools. Bennett's wit, poetic words, and loving thwacks upside the head are just what every creative person needs. Hearing her words is like sitting down with your best friend and receiving the advice your soul has been longing to hear."

— Amy Ahlers, author of *Big Fat Lies Women Tell Themselves*

"Whether you are just toying with the idea of pursuing a creative interest for the first time or you are already established in a creative field, *Get It Done* gets you excited to start prioritizing and pursuing your ideas. On top of that, Sam Bennett's exercises are actually enjoyable (as opposed to the kind that can feel like unpleasant homework) and will help you move your ideas out of your head and into the world. Bennett is refreshing in her positivity and achieves something rare — a how-to book that is funny and entertaining to read, and makes you feel good! Now, if you'll excuse me, I must go write an Oscar-winning screenplay. Or clean my room. One of the two — I'll figure it out."

— Rachel Dratch, cast member of *Saturday Night Live* and author of *Girl Walks into a Bar...*

"Within these pages, artists and nonartists alike will find brilliant, tangible tools to tap into their inner organizing genius. Even when it feels impossible, we all can create bits of time, and Bennett's strategies put fifteen minutes a day to superb use. This book is going to the top of my resource list for my creative clients."

— Marney K. Makridakis, author of *Creating Time*

"Fantastic for creative types of all stripes (actors, songwriters, visual artists, musicians, screenwriters), amateur, preprofessional, or professional. What Sam Bennett has to share is invaluable."
— Phil Swann, singer-songwriter, producer, author, and teacher

"Sam Bennett is the kind of insightful, articulate thinker who can make sense of the roadblocks we all face each day. Her book will help you get unstuck and on track, so that you can accomplish your goals."
— Clate Mask, cofounder and CEO, Infusionsoft

"Calling all artists! Are procrastination and perfectionism getting in the way of your sharing your creative gifts with the world? Through small, doable steps, *Get It Done* will help you make your big ideas real. Whether your roadblocks are limiting beliefs or challenges with money, time, and space, Sam Bennett has you covered with her real-world advice and time-tested tips."
— Jennifer Lee, author of *The Right-Brain Business Plan*

"I've been meaning to read Sam Bennett's book for a while, but I haven't done it yet. I'm sure it is very good."
— Charlie Hartsock, executive producer, *Crazy Stupid Love* and *The Incredible Burt Wonderstone*

GET IT DONE

GET IT DONE

FROM PROCRASTINATION TO CREATIVE GENIUS IN 15 MINUTES A DAY

SAM BENNETT

Foreword by Keegan-Michael Key

New World Library
Novato, California

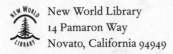 New World Library
14 Pamaron Way
Novato, California 94949

Text design by Tona Pearce Myers

Library of Congress Cataloging-in-Publication Data is available.

First printing, February 2014
ISBN 978-1-60868-210-2
Printed in Canada on 100% postconsumer-waste recycled paper

10 9 8 7 6 5 4 3 2 1

Contents

Exercises

Foreword

I was on a plane a few years ago and struck up a conversation with an average-seeming guy across the aisle who confessed to me that he was writing a memoir. Once we finished chatting, he pulled out a journal and started writing with unbridled joy. I heard him making audible gasps of discovery and revelation. It was as if a muse was sitting on his shoulder sharing an amusing anecdote every three seconds or so.

Needless to say, he was in the zone.

Given everyone's schedules these days, moments like this are rare. It seems as if an aluminum tube thirty-five thousand feet in the sky may be the only place where a person can find the reprieve necessary to have such a creative outburst. In my daily life, I can be working on four or five projects at a time and never feel like I'm giving enough attention to any of them.

The good news is that, according to Sam Bennett, we don't need to be literally airborne in order to create: we can soar in only fifteen minutes a day. Her easy-to-do approach made me feel absolutely invincible.

Sam has dedicated an enormous part of her life to helping us all deftly juggle our creative desires — the screenplay *and* the pottery kiln *and* the dance lessons (or, in my case, the martial arts classes). In the very near future — let's say the next twenty seconds or so —

you're going to dive into seemingly uncharted waters to find treasure that already belongs to you.

So have fun, don't *ever* let anyone tell you that you can't do it, and keep Sam around as your capable guide.

— Keegan-Michael Key, cocreator of *Key & Peele*,
writer, actor, and producer

Introduction

I began teaching the material in this book in 1996 or thereabouts —
for an "organized" person I'm remarkably hazy on dates and numbers — and called it the Get It Done Workshop. I've presented it
as a ninety-minute seminar, a three-week workshop, a twelve-week
workshop, a one-day intensive, and a six-week teleclass. The nice
thing is, the material seems to work every time.

I created all the exercises you'll find in this book in response to
the challenges I faced in my own peripatetic life as an actor, writer,
and teacher. Along the way, friends, colleagues, and students intro-
duced new questions, problems, and conundrums, and it was fun to
develop new ideas addressing their concerns.

After all, how do you move forward when there's no quarterly
review on how your novel's going?

When there's no raise or corner office to be earned by completing your one-person show?

When — frankly — no one cares if you move forward on your
projects but you?

As I continued to study the world of creative productivity, I
began to notice that while there were a lot of great books about getting organized out there (David Allen's classic *Getting Things Done*,
Julie Morgenstern's *Organizing from the Inside Out*, and Stephen
Covey's *Seven Habits of Highly Effective People* leap to mind), they

weren't exactly geared toward artists. Creative people don't care who's moved their cheese, you know?

The creativity books available (Julia Cameron's *The Artist's Way*, Mihaly Csikszentmihalyi's *Flow: The Psychology of Optimal Experience*, all of SARK's writings) seemed concerned with spiritual healing through creativity, or with the study of creativity, or with unleashing your inner creativity. But what about those of us whose creativity is already plenty unleashed, thank you very much? What is to become of us?

The problems facing creatives are the same regardless of discipline. Textile designers, singers, furniture designers, watercolorists — regardless of the medium, method, or genre, the issues remain the same:

How do I know which of my projects to pick?
How do I get started?
What if my idea is a dud?
What do I do when my perfectionism and self-doubt take over?
How do I manage my schedule and make time to do my work?
How do I keep going once my initial enthusiasm wears off?
How do I get my work out into the world?
What do I do if I hate marketing?
How do I handle criticism and praise?
How do I keep this up for my whole life?

It doesn't seem to matter if the creative person in question is a lifelong professional artist or a beginner just dabbling: the questions plaguing them are the same.

It turns out that movie stars, famous authors, award-winning artists, multiplatinum musicians, and your Aunt Martha the Crochet Queen all share the same self-doubt and the same problems getting work done. To wit: "I don't believe anyone ever suspects how completely unsure I am of my work and myself and what tortures of self-doubting the doubt of others has always given me" (Tennessee Williams). "Chefs are nutters. They're all self-obsessed, delicate, dainty, insecure little souls and absolute psychopaths. Every last one of them" (Gordon Ramsay).

Substitute any word you like for *chefs* in the above sentence, and you've got it.

Part of the problem is that you're weird and you know it. Whatever made you talented as a kid also served to make you a bit odd. Since, as my friend Sam Christensen has observed, you live in a world that constantly sends you conflicting messages — "Stand out! Fit in! Stand out! Fit in!" — it's hard to know how to behave. And no matter how many movies and sitcoms conclude with the simple, heartfelt message that you should "just be yourself," you walk around feeling lost, judged, and different — and not in a good way. "Among them but not of them," as Lord Byron said.

At the same time, you're a perfectly normal person with a job (or jobs) and a family and hobbies and the same quotidian concerns as everyone else on the planet. And so you worry that you're too normal and boring. You also possess other fascinating contradictions, such as:

- You care a lot about what other people think, and at the same time you don't give two figs about anyone else's opinion.
- You're a rebel and a rule breaker from way back, and you also would like to do things right. Bit of a perfectionist and an apple polisher, too, hmm?
- You spend a lot of time thinking about money and success, but you're not particularly motivated by those things. You like to work on the stuff that interests you, whether or not it pays.
- You are a gregarious loner.

- You are a people-pleasing iconoclast.
- You contradict yourself. You contain multitudes.

This book is about getting you back in touch with your creative power, navigating the tension between your apparent contradictions and giving you a little guidance as you blaze your own trail up the mountain of creativity.

There is no right way to use this book. There is only your way. Because you are an artist. Even if you feel a little uncomfortable calling yourself one, you are.

I believe that everyone is some kind of creative genius in her own peculiar way, and if you've ever been called sensitive, too sensitive, waaaaay too sensitive, weird, artsy, melodramatic, a big ol' drama queen, psychic, unique, odd, old-fashioned, eccentric, misguided, special, tolerant of ambiguity, optimistic, viciously self-critical, expressive, inventive, a Pollyanna, misunderstood, different, deluded, ambitious, contrary, talkative, awake, gifted, diverse, scary, intense, playful, iconoclastic, independent, freaky, unrealistic, or just plain crazy — then congratulations, you're an artist.

Reading this book is not like being in school. There are no rules and no grades and no way to do better or worse in this process. This is your life. You are the expert on you, and you will automatically do what's best and, moreover, what's right for you.

My mission with this book is to give you some support and inspiration around the projects that mean the most to you and, more important, to give you an opportunity to take a good, long, compassionate look at your creative process so you can figure out what's working, what can be jettisoned, and how to get out of your own way so your big genius-y ideas can get out into the world where they belong.

You can find downloadable versions of the exercises plus bonus audios and other materials here: www.GetItDoneBonus.com

xvi

One more word: I know how tempting it is to just read through a book like this and not do any of the exercises, but much like the stationery bicycle gathering dust in the garage, this book delivers much better results if you actually use it.

To summarize the suggestions I'll be making throughout the book:

- Discover which of your projects matters most to you.
- Rename that project.
- Spend fifteen minutes a day on that project, every single day.
- Get help and support from people who are genuinely helpful and supportive.
- Replace your fear and anxiety with cheerful curiosity.
- Track your progress.
- Celebrate your success.

So grab your favorite pen and some of that good paper you've got squirreled away, and let's get started investigating your big genius-y ideas and how to get moving on them *today*.

CHAPTER ONE

Procrastination Is Genius in Disguise

Have you ever noticed that procrastination causes you pain? It hurts your heart, it hurts your self-esteem, it hurts your relationships, it hurts your career, and it hurts your income. And just as a pain in your body alerts you to something that needs healing, the psychic pain of procrastination can serve as an important wake-up call. That is why I call procrastination genius in disguise.

If procrastination didn't hurt, then you could put stuff off and then just la-di-da around all carefree and happy. But that's not the way it works — when you put off your projects, they become a weight on your mind and your heart.

So why is that genius?

Because the pain caused by procrastination reminds you that your projects are important to you. Procrastination is your friend, tapping you on the shoulder and saying, "Hey, remember that idea you had? Remember how much you cared about it?" And pretty soon that voice is not just gently urging — it's nagging. Loudly.

So now you have a project that you know matters to you, and I'm going to guess it's mattered to you for a long time. After all this time, you are still thinking about it. It hasn't fallen away like some

> News flash: Nagging doesn't work. It doesn't work with your spouse, it doesn't work with your kids. And even *you* can't nag yourself into doing the projects that really matter to you. So if you catch yourself nagging a lot, pick another strategy.

1

things do — which is great news. The truth is, *procrastination is persistent desire.*

When your desire for a project stands the test of time, you can take that as a sign that your project truly is part of your life's calling.

What's Kept You from Moving Forward?

You've got a great idea that you know would make a difference in the world and it's stood the test of time so...what's the holdup? Why haven't you moved forward?

In my experience, there are three main reasons for getting stuck in procrastination.

Got Stuckified Reason 1: You Genuinely Don't Care about It

Maybe this project is really someone else's dream — a dream that your family or community placed on you — or maybe it's an old dream that you've outgrown.

Or perhaps it's something you think you should do. I call these "shadow goals." They look like goals, they sound like goals, but when you think about them they make you glum. Good goals are filled with energy and purpose — they may not always be fun, but they always contain some sense of joy. Shadow goals contain no joy but rather are burdened with guilt, ill feeling, futility, and even a bit of hopelessness.

For example, maybe you're telling yourself something like, "I should really go and get my master's degree." Chances are that if you have this idea and are not acting on it, you don't really care about a master's; you care about whatever you think having a master's will gain you: "If I got my master's in film I could write that screenplay I've had in my head." I say skip the master's and go directly to writing the screenplay.

It's also possible that you have outgrown this dream. It may be that while the fourteen-year-old version of you really wanted to be a rock star, the forty-four-year-old version doesn't actually care that much for the spotlight. If you are a sentimental person, you may feel it's unduly harsh to give up this particular project, because it may feel as though you are giving up on your dream. Allowing your old dreams to grow and change to better suit your true, current self is both practical and wise. Or to think of it another way, you wouldn't put your fourteen-year-old self in charge of your other life decisions now, would you?

> Your dreams are always a part of you, whether or not you fulfill them. Just like your memories and your fantasies, they cannot be taken away from you. You cannot abandon your dreams because your dreams never abandon you. But neither are your dreams entitlements. Live in dynamic relationship with your dreams, memories, goals, and ambitions and let them grow and change along with you.

Got Stuckified Reason 2: It Just Hasn't Been the Right Time

Maybe it hasn't been the right time because of life circumstances, such as a new baby in the family or a health issue or a financial crisis. Or maybe it hasn't been the right time because *you* haven't been ready. Maybe you've had life lessons to learn or some spiritual maturity to attain.

Or maybe it's that mysterious right-moment thing that people bring up when you're looking for the perfect life partner. "When the time is right, he/she will show up," those well-meaning people say. Irritating. Even more irritating, they are often correct.

Or maybe you've needed to wait for some technology to be invented, or you've needed to wait for the right people or the right partner. But whatever the reason: it just hasn't been the right time. *And I know that for a fact because if it had been the right time, you would have done it.*

After all, look at all the things you've accomplished. You're no slacker. You work hard, and you're so tenacious that others have probably expressed concern about your tenacity.

Got Stuckified Reason 3: You're a Little Bit Scared

Or a lot scared. To which I say, "Well, of course you're scared!"

Creating art is scary. Starting any new venture is scary. And putting your heartfelt work out into the world is downright terrifying. Anybody who claims otherwise is a big, fat liar. People tell me every day about the projects they're stuck on, and they are doozies. Here's a sample of some of the projects people have told me about:

Writing a memoir
Clearing up personal financials
Relearning quantum physics
Getting certified in a healing modality, such as massage, Reiki, Emotional Freedom Technique, or spiritual psychology
Balancing parenthood and art
Orchestrating a live event or conference
Getting a pilot's license
Living one's highest purpose
Doing stand-up comedy
Clearing out a parent's house
Staying in touch with friends and colleagues
Growing a business
Finding true happiness
Writing a book proposal

> I've been absolutely terrified every moment of my life — and I've never let it keep me from doing a single thing I wanted to do. — Georgia O'Keeffe

This is some big, life-changing stuff, and it's no surprise that it hits your panic button and makes you want to run and hide like a little kid.

I Know What I Need to Do — I Just Can't Make Myself Do It

Here's an example of the kind of letter I frequently receive from my clients:

I know what I need to do, I just can't make myself do it. I watch endless YouTube videos, I play computer solitaire, I fool around on Facebook — I even scrub my kitchen floors — all just to avoid the work that I know is my destiny. I get so mad at myself. Am I chasing a shadow goal? What do I do? — Elizabeth

Here's what I would say to Elizabeth, and to you, since chances are fairly high you are dealing with the same concerns:

Rest easy, honey — you are merely suffering from a biological imperative called "displacement activity." Displacement activity is what happens when an animal is in the grip of two conflicting instincts, and so it enacts a third, seemingly inappropriate behavior.

For example, you've probably seen a chimpanzee being challenged by another chimpanzee. When the first chimp doesn't know whether to run away or fight, he might scratch his head...yawn... look away...start grooming himself. Seems like a very passive response to aggression, but that chimp will do anything to deflect the energy, avoid making a decision, and otherwise make himself as invisible as possible.

When you have the instinct to create and you simultaneously have the instinct not to create, your fear says, "Don't do it!" And so, confused by these two equally strong instincts, you shut down and get stuck playing an online word game for hours on end.

Sometimes years.

It doesn't mean you have low self-esteem, and it doesn't mean your dream is impossible, and it certainly doesn't mean you're lazy. So the next time this happens, just recognize the dynamic without yelling at yourself. "Ah," you might say instead, "I appear to be having the instinct to create something. And I also find myself feeling afraid of what will happen if I create that thing. Perfectly natural. But my fear does not get to make my decisions for me. So I will now set my kitchen timer for fifteen minutes and just play around with my creative idea in a light, fun, beta-testing sort of a way and then see what happens."

And that's what this book is all about — giving you the loving encouragement you need to move forward. And maybe a little loving thwack upside the head.

We'll talk more in the next chapter about how to choose the right project, but here's a good shorthand tip: If you have lots and lots of ideas, you may want to pick one using the same method some people use to pay off their credit cards. That is, either pick the one that's closest to being done and finish that one, or pick the one that has the highest "interest" rate and finish that one.

Fifty years from now, the details that you are worrying about will not matter one whit. But the art you create, the novel you write, the doll you sew, the dance you perform, the photograph you take — that will still be making a difference in the world.

ACTION STEP

Spend fifteen minutes right now playing around with your favorite project.

CHAPTER TWO

Which of Your Thirty-Seven Projects to Tackle First?

You have so many great ideas, and you can't decide which one(s) to follow through on. Or maybe once you finally settle on one and get into it, you get bored and drop it like a hot potato for something new, I know.

One of the side effects of being a creative genius is that you have a billion great ideas and a lot of skills and talents, so it can be difficult to figure out where to focus. This is so often what happens: You get a brilliant idea. It appears instantly — so full and rich and detailed and vibrant inside your mind — and you just know it's a truly great idea.

And then — just as quickly — you feel stuck, overwhelmed, defeated. You have no idea how to move forward. Thinking about the thing in its entirety is just too overwhelming, so you get stuck before you've even started.

Here's the thing: your brain is a beautiful machine especially designed to look for patterns and solve problems. It works like a charm. Pose almost any question to your brain, and it will present you with an answer in no time at all. Genius, I tell you.

But if there are too many unknowns or too many variables, the machine grinds to a halt. Or it gets stuck in a loop, going around the same block over and over again. "I want to do X, but maybe I should do Y first, but I can't do that until I do Z, so maybe I shouldn't even try...but I really want to do X, but maybe I should do Y first..." Exhausting, right?

Breaking It Down

Let's say your big, beautiful idea is "I want to redo the whole house!" And you can see it! Gorgeous and gleaming. A full, rich, detailed vision of your house completely redecorated appears in your mind.

In this situation some people recommend creating a Vision Board, which I think is fun because I love gluing things onto other things. A Vision Board is a fun, artsy, self-actualization project — it's a collage you can make of images and words, usually cut from magazines, that, posted prominently, serves as a visual reminder of your goals and dreams. You can also make one online, which is fun, too. And if a Vision Board helps or delights or inspire you, then go ahead. But artists usually have no problem articulating a clear vision. Their vision is usually quite detailed and complete and often features sequels, theme parks, and a worldwide grassroots social movement.

> If you have some Vision Boards that are just hanging around making you feel bad about not having achieved your goals yet, for crying out loud, get rid of them. Inspirational tools are just that — tools to inspire you. The minute they quit inspiring you, lose 'em.

As you consider this beautiful vision of your redone home, you feel the gears in your mind begin to grind: Where to begin? How to afford it? Is now the right time? How do I know if a contractor is trustworthy? What if the paint comes out ugly? Where do I find those cool glass tiles? I don't know how to tile! *Ack!*

Too many unknowns and too many variables.

So if you can limit the scope of your project — take it bit by bit — you will be doing your brain a big favor. Tackling, say, just the carpeting in the upstairs bedroom will allow your brain to start searching its files for *carpet* in the same way that your computer can search for and find information easily once you give it the right name or search term. And now that your brain is whirring away on the idea of carpet, it might just remember that there's a carpet store over by the lunch place you like, and it might remember that your cousin Denise just redid her house — and maybe she'll have a few ideas for you — and hey, is that an ad for a carpet sale in today's paper?

Breaking your project down into manageable, bite-size bits makes it something you can actually *do*, as opposed to leaving it a big, overwhelming, untouchable vision that leaves you stuck. Think of it this way: *If you find yourself procrastinating, your project is too big!*

You can see how you might be able to make some real progress if you break you projects down into smaller chunks and spend a little time on them every day, yes? But this still leaves you with the all-important question, *How do you know which project is the right one?*

> We often downplay the importance of desire in our lives, but I have noticed that the things we really want to do pretty much get done. And the things we do not want to do pretty much do not get done. Have you noticed that, too?

For starters, you have to discern which of the projects matter most to you, and ditch the ones that don't. Here's a little quiz-type exercise that will help you do that.

 ### EXERCISE: FIVE QUICK QUESTIONS

Call to mind one of the many projects you are procrastinating on. I know you have lots, but for now, pick just one. Whichever one floats to the top of your mind first is fine.

Now — working swiftly and without pondering — answer *yes*, *no*, or *sort of* to these five questions:

1. Do you think you will learn from and enjoy working on this project?
2. Will completing this project make a difference in your life?
3. Will completing this project make a difference in the world?
4. Does your soul ache to work on it?
5. Ten years from now, will it matter whether or not you have done it?

Take a minute to muse on your answers, and jot down a few notes about what you notice. You may have noticed that those five questions are really one question, phrased five different ways — five different angles of attack on "Does this project truly matter?"

You may find that while you feel your project would make a big difference in the world, your soul does not ache to do it. That's okay. And that's important information for you to have if you decide to move forward: don't expect this project to make your soul sing. You may need to find some other spiritual sustenance while you're working on it.

Or perhaps you answered yes to every question but the first — that might be an indication that you need to find someone else, or gather a team, to execute this project.

But if you discovered that the project you were thinking about really doesn't matter to you, then for crying out loud — cross that project off your list or delegate it or something. There's no sense agonizing over a project you don't even care about.

Now think of another possible project, and repeat the exercise. In fact, repeat it until you have five possible projects that *definitely* matter to you. Feel free to pull projects from various areas of your life; this doesn't need to all be about your creativity. It's always a good idea to try it with at least one really crazy-daisy, dumb idea — even something you think is a *bad* idea. And you may also want to add in some "duty" options (like the voice in your head that says that you really should go back to school and get that advanced degree).

So now you have a list of five front-runner projects. Congratulations!

Your Pure Preference

One way to figure out which of these five projects to work on first is to determine your Pure Preference. Your Pure Preference is that which you really *want* to do. Desire is the gas in your creative tank. So getting in touch with that desire is the key to discerning your perfect project. To help you do just that, I have designed the Pure Preference worksheet (a.k.a. "You Cannot Chase Two Bunnies"). Before I describe the exercise further, I want to share some stories of clients who have used it.

LEAPS OF THE HEART: JERRY

I was working with a screenwriter named Jerry who was suffering from a terrible case of writer's block. When I asked him for a really crazy, bad idea to put on his list, he said, "Skydiving." And then he immediately added, "I don't know why I said that. I don't really want to go skydiving." I told him not to worry about it and just to trust the process of completing the exercise. After all, I assured him, he wasn't going to really have to do it.

As we worked through the list, every time we got to "skydiving" he would protest that he would never really go skydiving, that he had three kids and wouldn't do anything so dangerous. Again I encouraged him to just listen to his belly and keep answering based only on impulse.

When we got to the Total Your Score part of the exercise, Jerry was dismayed that skydiving had a high total score. "Listen," I said, "you're a writer — quit being so literal. Maybe the word *skydiving* doesn't mean actually jumping out of a plane. Maybe it means taking a wild leap in your work, or spiritually. Maybe your instincts are urging you to make an emotional skydive." He suddenly looked up at me. "My wife!" he said. "I think I need to propose to my wife all over again. We've grown a little distant since the kids were born, and I just realized that I want to feel that head-over-heels, jumping-out-of-a-plane feeling we had when we were first in love. It's risky, for sure — she might just laugh at me for being such a sop — but I really think I want to write her a love poem and ask her to marry me all over again."

Once I had dabbed up my mascara, I agreed. Who knew that one crazy-daisy, dumb idea could save a marriage?

SPEAKING OF MARRIAGE: IRENE

One time I was giving a workshop to a group at Leeza's Place, a nationwide organization that provides support to people with Alzheimer's and to their caregivers. The group consisted of eight people in their late sixties and seventies, most of whom were full-time caregivers to their terminally ill spouses or partners.

I gave them the Pure Preference exercise so that they could take a minute to figure out something they wanted to do for themselves. As you may know, getting a caregiver to focus on his or her own needs can sometimes be a bit of a challenge.

They were writing down the things they thought they

might want to do and tallying up their scores. It was all going swimmingly until Irene, a rather stern-looking woman in a jazzy tracksuit, said, "I don't see the point of all this."

"I mean," she said, "My number one thing is 'take a trip,' and I knew that would be my number one thing because I love to travel and I also know there's no way I can travel because I'm busy caring for my husband who's got Alzheimer's, and so what, I ask you, is the point of all this?"

"Well," I ventured, "sometimes it can be valuable to acknowledge that we want something we feel we can't have, and instead of being all good and brave about it, really let ourselves have the feelings of disappointment, rage, unfairness, and anger." Irene looked unconvinced.

"Also," I said, "I notice that number two on your sheet is 'go play bridge' — is it possible to think of that as a trip? You know, it's just a trip over to Studio City for a few hours, but it's still a trip, right? You know how you can convince a kid that going to the grocery store is a treasure hunt? I know it's sort of silly, but I find those little tricks can really help…" She wasn't buying it.

"You know," said Edgar, a round-faced gentleman at the end of the table, "Mary and I took a trip just last fall. We took a cruise down to Mexico. I picked a ship we'd been on before so that it would be a controlled environment and one that was somewhat familiar to her. We went with another couple so I didn't have to manage Mary all by myself, and we had a terrific time! It was only three days, but still — it was a trip!"

Before I could say anything, another woman chimed in. "Jeffrey and I went for lunch up to Santa Barbara last week, and that felt like a real vacation, too. I mean, we left at 11:00 AM and we were home by 4:00 PM, but it was as refreshing as a real vacation!"

Irene softened. "These are great suggestions," she said.

"Right," I said. "And notice how saying what you want — even though you thought it wasn't possible — got everyone's brain ticking along, coming up with creative solutions for you? *That's* the real value in determining what you want and saying it out loud."

Acknowledging what you really want and saying it out loud to other people — no matter how improbable fulfilling your desire may seem — not only gives voice to an important truth but also gets everyone thinking about creative ways that your goal might be met. Keeping your desire to yourself means that the only one working on it is you…and honey, you can't make all your dreams come true all by yourself.

Your Pure Preference is the project you would choose if money and time were no object, if your results were guaranteed, and if you knew for sure that no one's feelings would get hurt in the process. So now, without further ado, let us plunge into using this wonderful exercise.

EXERCISE: YOUR PURE PREFERENCE, A.K.A. "YOU CANNOT CHASE TWO BUNNIES"

At first glance, this exercise might seem a little complicated because of the numbers, but trust me, it's very simple and there's almost no math involved.

It uses what's known as a paired-comparison analysis, a great tool for sorting through a bunch of different options or for comparing apples to oranges. It is a delightfully subjective process, so don't try to think of all the "right" answers. Feel free to surprise yourself.

And let me also add that as important as your desire is in selecting your projects, it is not the only criterion. We're not trying to make a decision here, nor are we coming to any final conclusions. We're just getting one piece of the puzzle — the "your preference" piece.

Step 1. Compare Your Possible Projects in Pairs

Your list might look like this:

1. Write novel.
2. Make a five-minute film.
3. Move to Uruguay.
4. Start a blog.
5. Get a master's degree.

If you already know for sure what your project is, you might use this exercise to determine the best entry point or which piece of your project you'd like to tackle first.

For example, if you already know that you want to start a blog, your list might look like this:

1. Create a logo.
2. Choose a good name.
3. Make a list of possible topics.
4. Research similar blogs.
5. Hire a virtual assistant to help with the tech stuff.

Now comes the fun part: imagining that everything is perfect and yields great results. Imagine that you have stepped into a slightly parallel universe in which all things happen easily, and quickly, and that everything pays a million dollars. Everything comes with free parking and nice people and good snacks. Everything is covered in fairy dust, and even things that we know take time or effort somehow still seem easy and fun, okay? Got it? Good.

With your feet planted firmly in this imaginary world where everything works out perfectly, imagine that I am standing in front of you, and in one hand I have whatever you wrote down on line 1, and in the other I have whatever you wrote down on line 2. Which would you prefer? Go with your gut, and whichever number you prefer, circle the number in the pairing "1 or 2?" below. Then repeat this process for all the remaining pairs of numbers.

1 or 2?	2 or 3?	3 or 4?	4 or 5?
1 or 3?	2 or 4?	3 or 5?	
1 or 4?	2 or 5?		
1 or 5?			

Step 2. Total Up Your Scores

Tally up your results by counting how many times each number got circled as part of step 2, and record your results.

Step 3. Assess Your Results

Notice your results. Did something get zero votes? That's pretty common. And sometimes it means you honestly don't care about this project and that you should ditch it.

Sometimes it means that even though I've insisted we're in a magical land where everything is easy and profitable, you don't really believe me and the project is so fraught that you couldn't bring yourself to vote for it. In that case, you may need to put it on hold for now and do some more investigation and inner work as we move along.

Sometimes things that you *know* you have no desire to do but you have to do them anyway get zero votes. Taxes, for example. That's fine — acknowledging that you really don't want to do something can be an important step in getting it done. You can compensate for your lack of desire either by getting help or by promising yourself a big reward if you do it.

There may have been a clear winner — that's always nice. Sometimes the winner is surprising, and sometimes it's the thing that you knew all along was your favorite.

Often the list comes out a bunch of 2s and 3s — no real clear preference at all, which explains why you feel confused and muddied. You want a number of things equally. So now you can move on to looking at some of the other deciding factors, such as:

1. Which one has a real deadline and needs to be finished first?
2. Which one can you accomplish most easily?
3. Which one has the highest return on investment?
4. Which one fulfills your values most closely?
5. Which one seems like it would be the most fun?

Please note: this exercise is also a wonderful way to figure out where to go for dinner.

Now that you've determined which of your projects you'd like to start on first, here are two simple but profound exercises to kick you into high gear.

 ## EXERCISE: RENAME YOUR PROJECT

Give your project a new name. Because chances are you've either given it a horrible, homework-sounding name like "revise my manuscript" or "update the website," or you have been living with the name of this project for so long, it's become a sort of punishment every time you think about it.

Give it a fun name, a silly name, a sexy name, a name that makes you smile. "Work on my novel" sounds tedious, but "polish my diamond" sounds kinda fun; "send email about workshop" sounds tiresome, but "release a thousand kisses through the Internet" sounds kind of delicious.

One client, May, was trying to restart her acting career after taking time off to raise her kids. She found the whole concept of starting over depressing — it made her feel so old — that she couldn't bring herself to take the first step. When she renamed her project "finding center stage," she found that it fueled her love of acting and that it encouraged her to stay centered as she juggled motherhood and career.

And there's no need to be literal. Another client, Liza, called her project "embracing the mango" not because her project had anything to do with fruit, but just because that name felt yummy and sensual.

Gena was a successful television writer who wanted to transition into writing screenplays. When I urged her to rename her project, she demurred. "I don't know the name of the screenplay yet," she said. "No problem," I said. "When you think of creating this screenplay, what verb comes to mind other than *writing*? *Dancing*? *Flirting*? *Singing*?" "Birthing," she said without hesitation. "Great," I said, "and if your screenplay were a color, what color would it be?" She looked straight at me and said, "Blue." "Perfect! We'll call your project 'birthing blue.'"

Working swiftly, write down a few possible names for your project, and pick one that tickles your fancy, challenges you, or has a mysterious appeal.

EXERCISE: MAKE A "COULD-DO" LIST

Get out a piece of paper and write "Could Do" at the top.

I like "could-do" lists because I find "to-do" lists too dictatorial. They make me feel pressured and antsy and reluctant and even belligerent — like a pouting high schooler who's being harassed to do her homework. But the words *could do* put me in a place of choice.

I could do the laundry, or I could walk around in dirty, smelly clothes. I have a choice. Even if the task is something I know I must do, I feel more relaxed if I remember that I have the option to not do it.

Plus, we're not trying to think of things that you will do for sure; we're just brainstorming things that you *could* do. Maybe you will, and maybe you won't — we don't know yet. We'll just have to see how you feel.

We'll talk more about managing your lists in chapter 5, but for now, here are some suggestions about where to start your own could-do list.

1. *Write down the name of a person who could really help you out on this project.* Maybe it's someone you know, maybe it's a hero who inspires you, or maybe it's someone from ancient history who could serve as an imaginary guide. You might also want to make a note about how this person could be of assistance. Could she give you advice? Introduce you to someone? Cheerlead? Proofread?

2. *Write down the name of someone who will not help you out on this project.* Maybe it's someone who will be

"Could-do" lists give you the room to write down any old idea, no matter how silly or improbable. Sometimes writing down an action step that you would never take, not even in a million years, can inspire a great idea that you're really eager to follow up on. For example, you might write down, "call famous celebrity chef for endorsement," and while that idea might feel ridiculous and impossible, it could inspire you to connect with a local caterer, restaurateur, or food journalist. And there's always the chance that you'll find a way to connect with that famous celebrity chef. Funny how things like that happen...

I have noticed that while people are fairly indifferent to generalized requests, long sighs, martyred glances, and vague complaining, specific requests such as "Could you give me dialogue notes on act one?" or "Could you recommend a good watercolor instructor near downtown Portland?" are usually responded to swiftly and in the affirmative.

helpful to you down the road (but not right now), or someone who is always a big ol' Debbie Downer. Regardless,
take a moment to think about the person with whom you
will *not* discuss your project today.

Notice that it doesn't mean that you don't love him,
admire him, value his opinion, whatever — it just means
that as of today, you are going to consider the option of
keeping this project out of his sticky, sticky hands.

3. *Write down one simple, easy, and affordable step you might
    take toward working on your project.* This should be some-
    thing that will take you less than fifteen minutes and that
    you can very easily afford. That's right — I'm talking baby
    steps.

What is one tiny, incremental gesture you might make toward
your project today? Is there:

- something you could research?
- some tool you could buy or borrow?
- some doodle or outline you could sketch out?
- some phone call or email you could easily execute?

Yep. That's all there is to it. If you write down one small thing
you can do every morning (*before* checking your email) you will
make astounding progress and — bonus — you will feel *great*.

Because as much as procrastination hurts your heart, moving
forward — even just a little, tiny bit — makes your heart sing.

ACTION STEP

Tell a supportive friend or colleague about your project, and ask
them for any encouraging ideas, insights, or suggestions.

CHAPTER THREE

Your Creativity Toolkit

I am inspired by new tools and practices, but then I often hit resistance to using them. What can I do? — Leonard

Planning makes me rebel against my plans. Yes! Making plans brings out the rebel, "you can't make me" part of my personality. So the plans don't happen. — Nora

I'd be super-grateful if you could share one or two of your most magical motivation makers for especially stubborn geniuses. — Geri

Sometimes we resist new practices because they really aren't the right thing for us, and sometimes we resist because they *are* the right thing for us and we're just being stubborn about making a change.

I don't think there's a quick way to tell the difference between these two kinds of resistance ahead of time. You just have to plain old dive in and try a new practice for a few weeks. If it works, great. If it doesn't, you may be able to tweak it and make it better, or it may inspire some totally different strategy that's perfect for you.

Aside: The Story of Jess and the Giant Journal

Jess is a tall, articulate fellow who looks and acts like a writer. Which is fortunate, because he is a writer. A few years ago

21

he tried doing the "morning pages" as prescribed in Julia Cameron's *The Artist's Way*. While this admirable daily writing practice has helped countless artists have meaningful breakthroughs, Jess's experience was a little different: "It made me crazy. I absolutely hated it. I forced myself to do them every day for over a month, and every single morning all I could think was, 'This is boring. If I write bigger, could I fill up three pages faster, or is that cheating?'" Finally, Jess realized that the morning pages were boring to him because, as a writer, putting together words to describe what was happening was something he did automatically. It felt redundant to write out what was, essentially, already written in his mind.

What he needed was to *express* his feelings — not explain them. So he got himself a big drawing pad of newsprint and a new box of magic markers, and every morning he would scrawl a picture of how he was feeling. He made no attempt to create artwork; he just wanted to get his internal life out on paper. No one would ever see it, and the paper was cheap, so he felt he afford to fail, he could afford to be truthful, and he could afford to be over-the-top in the visual expressions of his feelings. Sometimes he drew his dreams; sometimes he made signs; sometimes he drew cartoons. Sometimes he drew himself; sometimes he drew others. He drew his goals, he drew his fears, and he drew his prayers.

"All this time," he told me, "I thought I was a failure for not being able to keep a journal. Turns out all this time the journals were just too small."

So here are some of the daily practices that have worked for me and for countless clients, and while I urge you to try them as written just to see what happens, please feel free to amend them in whatever way works best for you.

Nearly Miraculous Daily Habits

Here are the top three Nearly Miraculous Daily Habits that will support you in becoming a fully expressed, productive creative genius. I have noticed that my clients and students who embrace these habits usually see jaw-dropping, life-changing results.

> Plunging into your day knowing that you've already made even a little bit of progress on the work that is dearest to your heart will improve your whole world.

Nearly Miraculous Daily Habit 1:
Allot Fifteen Minutes a Day to Your Project

If I could actually make you do stuff, the first thing I would get you to do is to spend fifteen minutes each and every day working on your project. As it happens, you are the agent of change in your life, and I can't really make you do anything. But I strongly urge you to make this daily commitment to your project.

Try fifteen minutes every morning — before you check your email, before you check your email, BEFORE YOU CHECK YOUR EMAIL — working on your project. You will need an iron will to resist the siren call of the Internet, but it's worth it. Whatever's out there can wait while you put yourself first for just a few minutes. (One client found that if she turned off her browser when closing her computer at night it was easier for her to avoid distraction when she came back to write in the morning.)

So get out your kitchen timer, or use the timer on your cell phone (in which case you can select an alert sound that you particularly enjoy), and even if you just sit still for fifteen minutes, you will profit. I've heard from my students with attention deficit disorders that using a timer is an especially useful focusing ritual.

You will be amazed by how much work you can get done in fifteen minutes. You will be flat-out astonished by how much progress you make by putting in fifteen minutes a day, seven days a week, for a week, for a month, for three months, for a year.

Intellectually, this makes perfect sense. You know that if you practiced guitar every day for fifteen minutes, before long you'd be a better guitar player. If you spend fifteen minutes a day writing a novel, eventually you will have written a novel. If you spend fifteen minutes a day working on your abs, pretty soon you'll have strengthened your core.

But emotionally this strategy doesn't feel like it will work. It feels too small and too half-baked. It may also trigger some feelings of rebellion, anger, despair, or fatigue. Sometimes those feelings show up right when you're on the verge of a breakthrough.

You might want to think of this as your Daily Fifteen Minutes of Fame. It's your chance to treat yourself like a famous artist for fifteen minutes every day. After all, would a famous artist have any trouble claiming this small amount of time for herself? Of course not.

Maybe you're thinking, "Okay, Sam, but how do I go about this fifteen-minute thing?" Here's what I recommend:

Your Daily Fifteen Minutes of Fame — the Why

Quickly — without pondering — close your eyes for a moment and ask yourself, "What does this project represent for me? What *value* of mine does it represent?" and just let the answer bubble up from inside. Maybe your answer will be "freedom" or "joy" or "self-expression" or "love" or "escape from the cubicle" or "to prove everybody wrong" — whatever word or phrase brings a little smile to your face is the right one.

You might even make yourself a little sign with your word or phrase on it and post it on or near your timer. (You could even grab a paint pen and decorate your kitchen timer if you were so inclined — a bit of glitter and glue, anyone?)

Your Daily Fifteen Minutes of Fame — the What

Working swiftly, brainstorm a list of fifteen-minute tasks. Include a wide variety, since some days you might wake up feeling bold and want to tackle something brave such as "entering poetry contest," and on others you'll feel quiet and shy and want to do something simple like doodling or daydreaming. With this list at hand, you can quickly select the task that matches your mood.

For example, if I were writing a play called *Romeo and Juliet*, my list of fifteen-minute tasks might look something like this:

- Write a quickie character sketch of the nurse.
- Research poisons and sleeping draughts.
- Work on the balcony scene.
- Call agent.
- Brainstorm titles (*Capulet vs. Montague, Why Fifteen-Year-Old Girls Should Not Be Allowed to Go Dancing Unchaperoned*)
- Write an author's bio for the back cover.
- Double-check penalties for dueling.
- Write a blog post about doing the wrong thing for the right reasons.
- Research whether a rose by any other name really *would* smell as sweet.

Your Daily Fifteen Minutes of Fame — the When

I usually suggest working in the morning, just because getting stuff out of the way first thing seems to work for a lot of people, including myself, but you might find that working after school works well (family homework time?) or just before bedtime. Some people like to work in the middle of the night. Experiment.

LUNCHTIME PLAYS

My friend Emilie Beck is an award-winning playwright and theater director, and once she wrote a play (two plays, actually) in twenty-minute increments. She had two small boys at home and a very demanding full-time job, and twenty minutes each day during her lunch hour was truly the only time she had. It was not her preferred method of working, to be sure, but she made the best of it.

She found not only that she was able to do some great work but also that the action of writing every day helped remind her of her life goals, and kept her in touch with her artist-self, which was, I imagine, in danger of getting temporarily swallowed up by her mommy-self and her executive-self.

LESLEY'S STORY (IN HER OWN WORDS)

I will be honest, I didn't believe you at first. You were so adamant about how only fifteen minutes a day can help you complete a project. "Yeah, right," kept sounding in my head. It was that same voice that always held me back from starting a project because I never knew where to start.

Whether I was starting a necklace or a painting, I always felt that if I started it, then I would have to finish it right then and there. That is a lot of pressure, so I would sometimes just shrug off some great ideas. I figured I had nothing to lose by following your advice.

I set the timer on my cell phone and started a necklace right away. It took me three fifteen-minute sessions to complete one, but by the end of the week, I had three more necklaces than I had anticipated. I filled in my fifteen minutes with production, and I started to value what fifteen minutes can bring you in a day, a week, and a month! So I decided to transfer this wisdom to my paintings.

Sometimes I would feel inspired to go longer than fifteen minutes. However, if I had only fifteen minutes to give to a project, I was okay with it.

What I am sharing with you today is a painting that I started in February 2011 and finally completed it August 2011. This painting is very meaningful to me and expresses the journey that I have embarked on since starting the fifteen-minutes-a-day process.

The background is a tile collage of different tattoo images that I found in various tattoo magazines (during my fifteen minutes a day I would skim through magazines and cut out my favorite images). Soon I had collected enough to fill up the canvas (again, in different fifteen-minute segments, I glued them to every quadrant of that canvas). Once the canvas was filled, I started painting the woman. (In those fifteen-minute segments I learned how to get the skin tones I liked, and I played with shadow.)

I will be honest: sometimes during my fifteen-minute segments I would just stare at the canvas and try to figure out what my next move would be. But those fifteen minutes of thought are what helped bring about the spiderweb, the filigree, and the crystals, all of which helped me complete this painting.

> I call this painting the Stuntwoman, which is something you once called me. I have found balance in my life, in my career, by just appreciating fifteen minutes every day.

An image of Lesley's painting can be found here: www.The OrganizedArtistCompany.com/?p=1041

By the way, I gave Lesley the stuntwoman idea because once as she was talking to me about feeling overwhelmed by her schedule, I suggested that she consider the idea of being busy without buying into the story that busy equals being stressed out: "Think about being busy in the same way that a surgeon is busy during an operation," I told her. "Be busy like a trapeze artist flying through the air, or like a stuntwoman — just cleanly moving through each task with great clarity, concentration, and grace."

Nearly Miraculous Daily Habit 2: Find an Idea Catcher

You are a genius, and you have a lot of really good ideas every day. But chances are, you're not writing them down. And the life span of an unrecorded idea is...well, it's pretty short.

Paying attention to your creativity causes increased creativity.

So find a system that works for you, and use it every day. I like writing my ideas on index cards because they are cheap and cheerful and easy to carry.

But there are lots of other methods:

- Carry a little notebook.
- Use a voice memo app on your phone.
- Create an area in your datebook or journal for ideas.
- Find a note-taking app that you love to use.
- Call yourself and leave a message.

- Write on Post-its and stick them in places where you'll see them.

- Use a coupon-carrier type envelope in which you can file your little scraps of paper

If you're not a write-things-down kind of person, you might want to try tapping your wrist, forehead, or sternum as you repeat the idea out loud several times, or you might try turning your idea into a little song you can sing to yourself. These kinds of mnemonics work beautifully for some people.

Then you need to create a home for these great ideas. (Here is my most succinct organizational tip: everything needs the right-sized home.) For your random ideas or for the ones you are not moving forward on, I suggest creating a file, folder, or envelope, and labeling it "Genius." At the end of each day, put your ideas in there. They will nest and grow and, eventually, turn into something fabulous.

Index cards helped me write this book.

When I first had the idea for this book, I thought it was great, but I also got immediately stuck because I wasn't sure what format the book should be in. Should it be a workbook? A thought-for-the-day book? A six-week plan with prescriptive exercises for each day?

I knew I was falling into the trap of believing that I needed to have it all perfect inside my head before I moved forward, so I decided to let this book tell *me* what it wanted to be. For several weeks, every time I had an idea for something that I thought should be in the book, I wrote it down on an index card and put it in a "My Brilliant Book" manila envelope. After about six weeks of this, I spread all the index cards out on my dining room table and began to sort them. I played around with a few different ways of organizing the ideas and finally ended up with a structure I really liked.

The fun part came when I started writing in earnest. Whenever

I got stuck or didn't know what part of the book to work on, I would just reach my hand into the envelope and write about the idea on whatever index card I pulled out. I loved letting chance and fate have a hand in my daily writing practice.

Nearly Miraculous Daily Habit 3:
Allot Fifteen Minutes a Day for Deliberate Daydreaming,
a.k.a. Great Thoughts in the Shower

I have a tiny suspicion that someday, far in the future, people will look back at our ideas about the right brain–left brain dichotomy and laugh. I suspect they will find this brain theory of ours ridiculously primitive, and they will wonder at our lack of understanding, in much the same way that today we cringe at outdated medieval medical practices.

A body in motion puts the mind in motion.

But for the time being, the right brain–left brain model is the best understanding that we have. For those not familiar with it, let me give you the most basic outline. Different parts of the brain appear to be in charge of different functions. The left hemisphere is thought to be responsible for logic, language, and analytical, step-by-step thinking. The right hemisphere is thought to be responsible for intuition, visual design, and holistic, big-picture thinking.

Of course, no one is only right- or left-brained. But you may recognize yourself dwelling more in one camp than in the other. And you may be slightly relieved to know that your tendency to process information verbally (causing your mother to describe you as a chatterbox) or your tendency to get caught up in the flow of something and lose track of time is not disobedience on your part but rather a function of how your brain works.

Many artists find themselves heavily favoring their right brain, but even so, artistic blocks caused by left-brain intervention occur even to the best of us. Writer's block, musical ruts, creative impasses: everyone feels stymied at one time or another.

So there you are, trying to let your ideas blossom while your left brain is standing there tapping its foot and saying, "This old dumb thing again? Didn't you do this already? Remember what that one critic said about your work — don't you want to take her notes into account? Is this going to sell? Aren't you done yet?" And so forth. And, you know, that voice sounds so darned *logical*. Perhaps that voice is right. Maybe it is time for you to give up all this tomfoolery once and for all.

Now, maybe it's time to give up all this tomfoolery, and maybe it isn't. But the fact of the matter is that right now you're trying to get some work done and you're stuck. The trick is to give your logical, linear, left brain something interesting to do while your right brain gets to do its impulsive, elliptical, intuitive work.

You want your hands to be busy so your mind can wander.

Deliberate daydreaming has beneficial effects in increased creativity, concentration, and stress reduction. I think of it as giving your brain a little quiet time so that it can deliver ideas, dreams, and answers without getting drowned out by your daily mental chatter.

Do some simple, repetitive motion for fifteen minutes a day, every day. But this is not to get fit or to lose weight or to lower your blood pressure — it's to enhance your creativity and turn up the volume on your intuition. Find some exercise that you don't mind doing — walking, running, swimming, doing calisthenics, dancing, jumping rope — and find time for it every single day. If your energy level or range of motion is impaired, you can knit, toss cards into a hat, chop vegetables, fold laundry, sort papers, or even go for a drive.

Any repetitive task tends to occupy the left (logical) brain just enough for the right (creative) brain to flower. That's why you always have such great ideas in the shower or while you're out walking the dog. So it's time to cultivate that habit.

You need to make an every-day commitment in order to automate your decision making and free yourself up from the internal debate that sounds like "Should I walk today? I walked yesterday. But I might not walk tomorrow. And it might rain. I'm sort of tired." That debate is just a big energy drain.

Tell yourself that you're going to do it every day, and then do it. No excuses. You don't have to do it well — feel free to make a halfhearted effort. And let me reiterate: this is *not* for your health. It is for your creativity and your creativity alone. (Although, of course, inspired daily motion is great for you, so there may be some delightful fringe benefits!)

Here are a few how-to-do-it suggestions:

- Go for a walk. Amble, even. Human beings were designed to walk, and I believe that the pattern our bodies make when we're walking stimulates brain activity in a very positive way.

- Go for a walk and count something. If you're out walking and you still can't make a breakthrough, start counting. You can count your steps or your breaths or the lampposts or anything regular. The counting keeps your left brain occupied so that your right brain is free to conceive new ideas. Counting works great while jumping rope, swimming, or doing sit-ups, too.

- Take a shower. Let your left brain soap, rinse, and repeat (you know you don't really have to repeat, right? — that's just a way for the shampoo people to sell more shampoo) while your right brain gets to enjoy the warmth, hear the white noise of the water, relax, and receive inspiration.

- Bake cookies. Make soup. Create a perfect chopped salad by dicing the vegetables exactly the same size. If you like cooking, you'll love the quiet, relaxing feeling that comes over you as your hands and left brain conspire to create delicious food, leaving the rest of you to do some productive whole-picture thinking.

- Pitch pennies. Play marbles. Make something out of pipe cleaners or Play-Doh.
- Go for a drive. If you enjoy driving, fill up the tank and take off. Don't listen to music — just drive. Don't worry. You won't get lost, and you might just get found.
- Go fishing.
- Practice another discipline. I'm guessing that you're good at some other art form. This is the time to break out that knitting, head over to the woodshop, rinse off the paint brushes, play the lute, and give yourself a little creative vacation.
- Paint by numbers. That's right. Paint by numbers. It's better than taking tranquilizers and has fewer calories than liquor. There is a meditative aspect to painting by numbers that is unmatchable. Give it a try! If anyone catches you at it, say you're engaging in a postironic commentary on the commercialization of color and the homogenization of form in a consumer-based society.
- Just get up and turn around. From wherever you are, I want you to stand up and face the other direction. Amazing thoughts and breakthroughs can slip into

> Fishing for trout is like having a career in the arts. Why? Because while good equipment can help, it's no guarantee that you'll catch anything. And just because you caught something yesterday doesn't ensure that you'll do it again today. Or ever. Amateurs can often do just as well as pros, and children can often beat them both. And in the end, if you are going to fish, the reward mustn't be the fish, or even the promise of fish.
>
> The reward must be found in the process of standing on the shore in all kinds of weather, loving each cast.

your brain when you are willing, quite literally, to change your perspective.

Notice that all these suggested daily activities are nonnarrative. There are no stories or even language involved in any of these activities. So that means no TV, no video games, no reading, no movies, and no Internet.

Just fifteen minutes of deliberate daydreaming.

Every Field Must Lay Fallow

Maybe none of the above will work for you. Maybe you are in the middle of a dry spell so severe your lips are parched. I'm sorry. I know that feeling — that sinking, empty, aching feeling — and I wouldn't wish it on anyone. But I know that eventually it will end. And you will live through it. I'm sorry I can't say how long "eventually" will be, but I do know that you will get your mojo back.

You are an artist. And sometimes artists endure extended periods during which it seems as if nothing's happening. It's called *acedia*, meaning "spiritual torpor and apathy; ennui" or "anomie in societies or individuals, a condition of instability resulting from a breakdown of standards and values or from a lack of purpose or ideals."

And it doesn't mean you're dead inside. It just means that you've temporarily lost the ability to feel joy in your work. Which is sad.

If you find yourself in a hole, stop digging. Being creatively stuck is a miserable experience, and sometimes, when the going gets tough and the well goes dry, artists think this is the time to really buckle down. And they force themselves to stare at an empty page or recite lines that sound like nonsense. I'm here to say: that almost never works.

Do hard work when hard work is required. But sometimes taking a productive, intentional break from your labors can refresh you and lead you to new, better work. I'm not saying goof off; I'm saying respect the rhythm of your creativity.

But if you accept this dry spell as a stage in the artistic process, feeling fully confident that no one and nothing can ever take away your identity as an artist (after all, they haven't been able to make it go away yet, have they?), you just might survive.

Maybe this is the time to pursue some of those other things you always say you want to do. Volunteer more. Have lunch with friends. Take a temporary job in a field that's of interest to you. Spend more time with children. Read all those books you've got piled up. Plan a trip. Sit on the couch with the television off.

Whatever happens, don't give up on yourself.

Eventually you will get a little tickle. An idea will whisper to you. You'll catch yourself thinking, "I wonder if..." and you'll be off to the races again, productive, happy, and rejoicing in the renewal of your vibrant, creative voice.

Tracking Your Progress

One of the most important things you can do to enhance your happiness is to notice your progress. As Tony Hsieh, author of *Delivering Happiness* and CEO of Zappos.com, puts it, "Happiness is really just about four things: perceived control, perceived progress, connectedness (number and depth of your relationships), and vision/meaning (being part of something bigger than yourself)."

But it's actually very difficult for us to discern our own progress. After all, we're hunter-gatherers, so we're always on to the next thing. You're not even done with breakfast before you start thinking about lunch. And when you do notice what you've accomplished, you mostly notice what's wrong with it or what you would do better the next time.

A little structure can go a long way here: keeping track of your progress is a great way to notice what's working, what problems are recurring, and where you might just want to leave well enough alone.

 EXERCISE: WEEKLY PROJECT TRACKING

I created the Weekly Project Tracking sheet below to help me notice and celebrate my progress. Make your own by simply dividing a piece of paper into four quadrants and adding the headings in each quadrant. Then fill it in according to the guidelines that follow.

WEEKLY PROJECT TRACKING	
5 Accomplishments I'm Proud of from the Past Week: 1. _____ 2. _____ 3. _____ 4. _____ 5. _____	What Do I Know Now That I Didn't Know Then? _____ _____ _____ _____
The Critical, Rational Voice Tells Me: _____ _____ but My Inner Wisdom Says: _____ _____ _____	3 Things I Could Do This Week: 1. _____ 2. _____ 3. _____

Upper Left-Hand Quadrant:
5 Accomplishments I'm Proud of from the Past Week

In the upper left-hand quadrant, you can list wins from any area of your life. They may be related to your project — I mean, that is kind of the idea — but you have a whole life to live, too. If you were writing and orchestrating a song, your list might look like this:

1. Wrote out melody & lyrics.
2. Added rhythm section.
3. Added backgrounds.
4. Assigned backgrounds to particular instruments.
5. Double-checked for balance and errors.

Another week you may have family in town, and so your list might look like this:

1. Took the folks to the Contemporary Art Museum. (Note: It's fun to be a tourist in my own town!).
2. Had a lovely dinner with the folks.
3. Did not go crazy when the folks started suggesting I get a "real" job.
4. Asked the folks a bunch of questions about my grandparents — fascinating!
5. Wrote a poem inspired by my family history.

Other weeks you may feel unwell, or you may be wrestling with a personal problem or recovering from heartbreak, and so your list might look like this:

1. Got a lot of rest.
2. Canceled my book group meeting.
3. Had the housekeeper come in and clean.
4. Went for a long walk.
5. Took an extra day off and didn't answer the phone all day.

The idea is that you take a moment to notice what's going *right* in your life, whatever that means for you right now.

Ninety-Nine Compliments and One Criticism

You know how sometimes you'll do something and everyone loves it and says such nice things to you, and then one person says one thing that's a tiny bit critical and then that's all you hear?

Yep. Me, too.

That phenomenon is not the result of having low self-esteem or anything. It's a perfectly natural and instinctive human response called "negative bias," and it just means that we're programmed to remember the bad stuff more than the good. It's a survival mechanism, because it's much more important for our brains to remember the one berry that made us sick than the ninety-nine delicious berries. And it's much more important for us to remember the behavior that got us in trouble with the tribe than it is to remember the specifics of our approved-of behavior. So we need to fight nature a bit here and deliberately turn our attention to the ninety-nine delicious berries.

When you start to make a list of the five things you're proud of from last week, don't be surprised if you find yourself thinking, "Nothing! I did nothing in the past week that I feel even a little bit proud of. I can't even *remember* last week." That's very common. Just take a deep breath, maybe take a look at last week's calendar, and start small. List only things that genuinely give you a feeling of pride and accomplishment. Remember, no one need ever see this, so feel free to be completely idiosyncratic in how you define a win.

Notice how tracking your weekly wins starts to affect your drive, your confidence, and your productivity. Imagine having fifty-two of these sheets chronicling your year. That feels good, hmm?

Upper Right-Hand Quadrant:
What Do I Know Now That I Didn't Know Then?

Originally I used the upper right-hand quadrant to track project-related research, so I would write down things such as, "I learned that XYZ costs more than I expected it to" or "I learned that studies show that students of the arts in all disciplines outperformed their nonarts peers on the SAT by 91 points in 2009."

As I began to share this Weekly Project Tracking sheet with my clients and students, I noticed that they often liked to record new things they had learned about themselves.

One student, Claire, was tremendously shy and soft-spoken. In surprising contrast to her Edwardian, delicate-violet demeanor, she really wanted to get into comedy writing, so we created a project for her that, in part, involved her beginning classes at the Second City (my comedy alma mater).

Now, if you've ever taken an improvisation class, you know how boisterous and outrageous those classes can be, and I was concerned that Claire might get sort of... trampled.

The week of her first class she reported the following to me in her sweet, piping voice: "I learned that I really like improvising and I really like comedy, and I learned that even though I get nervous, my fears do not get to make my decisions for me."

Now, that's success!

> **Your fear does not get to make your decisions for you.**

Lower Left-Hand Quadrant:
Critical, Rational Voice versus Inner Wisdom

You know that logical-sounding voice in your head that discourages you? The one that says things like, "No one sells a first novel," or, "All the good ones are taken, married, or gay," or, "In this economy?" This voice may be the voice of an actual person you know, or it may just be a voice in your head. Either way, take a minute to listen to it and write down what it's saying, word for word, in the lower left-hand quadrant of the worksheet.

Now take a breath and think about your life. What evidence do you have that contradicts that voice? I'm not looking for generic affirmations here, nor do I want baseless optimism. I want you to think of some actual, honest statement that is true.

You might think, "Well, it's possible that first novels are a tough sell, but I know I often have great beginner's luck." Or, "Yes, some people may have trouble finding a partner, but I notice that I've always had a love interest when I've wanted one." Or, "Some people may be struggling in this economy, but I also notice lots of people prospering. Maybe I could prosper, too." Write down those words here, too.

See how it feels to give that calm, knowing voice of your inner wisdom a chance to speak. You may want to keep those honest words of encouragement nearby during the week.

Lower Right-Hand Quadrant:
3 Things I Could Do This Week

Three. Just three.

I know — your list is a mile long. But I want you to think of three things that would give you a true feeling of accomplishment, that would make a difference to you or to someone else, that you would love to write down in the "5 Accomplishments That I'm Proud of from the Past Week" section next week, and write them here, in the lower right-hand quadrant.

Stay on the sharp edge of possible. Challenge yourself, but don't make any task so hard or complicated that you can't do it.

And again, this is *your* list, so there may be things on here that no one else would notice or care about. That's fine. You may want to make sure you get eight hours of sleep each night, or perhaps you want to research that publisher your friend mentioned.

You're looking for three goals that inspire you, shake you up a bit, make you smile, or tantalize you.

Try to avoid goals inspired by that stern, critical, rational voice, okay? If you feel tired or discouraged before you've even started, or if there's even a whiff of "loser" to it, you're probably dealing with a shadow goal. So just take a moment to reconnect with that inner wisdom and find something more delicious to achieve.

Of course you'll want to make this tracking sheet your own. Rearrange it, decorate it, swap out the categories if you like. You may want to add some particular metric or other, such as tracking your income, spending, or calories, or maybe you want to create a doodling space to record the images that come to you in meditation.

Whatever works for you today is right.

ACTION STEP

Make a quick list of potential fifteen-minute tasks.

CHAPTER FOUR

Overcoming Perfectionism

If it can't be perfect, why would I even begin? — Mark

I start something, but then I tinker with it forever and never finish it. — Lauren

I just get so frustrated because I know it'll never be as perfect in real life as it is in my mind. — John

Perfectionism is an insidious demon that must be fought with every weapon you've got. Here's what's so tricky about perfectionism: it (sort of) turns procrastination into a virtue.

Because it's good to have high standards, right?

And it's good to expect the best from yourself, right?

We want to make things that are beautiful, unique, extraordinary...

And then you crumble under the pressure you've put on yourself and never create anything at all. But it's not your fault — it's your damned high standards.

Perfectionism also keeps you from noticing the great things that you create effortlessly. By keeping your focus on that which is hard, unattainable, or impossible to execute, you fail to give yourself credit for that which is easy and fun. While you're busy struggling with the idea that you need to be a great painter (all the while *not* painting), you might miss out on a brilliant career as a caricaturist. Your frustrated desire to write the perfect novel can prevent you from seeing your potential as a lyricist.

This is the worst kind of snobbery. Disdaining your own gifts is as cruel as disdaining your own children.

My friend and client Patti Frankel once confided to me that she had three unpublished novels sitting in her desk drawer. *Three!* And they languished there because even though she had gotten good feedback from other writers and even from a literary agent, she felt that the warm, funny, romantic novels that she loved to write weren't "significant" enough. "I'm really smart," she told me. "And I thought that smart women were supposed to get their PhDs and help save the world, you know? But I don't want to save the world that way. I just want to write books that make people feel good." She had thought that it was more important for her to slog along completing a PhD that, it turned out, she didn't care very much about. So after our first session she made the radical decision to let it go, two courses and half a dissertation away, and to give her heart and soul to the novel that was so dear to her. She just let me know that she's finished it and is now working with an editor.

Quick — think of the most extreme, avant-garde artist you can name. Now think of a boring, middle-of-the-road artist. If there's room in the world for both of them to be famous, there is certainly room for you.

Once you actually begin working, the first thing you will need to surrender is your idea about who you are and what your work is about.

You will also need to quit waiting to feel ready. To quit waiting for it to be perfect. To quit your big ideas about what's good and what isn't and what people will pay for and what they won't.

Don't Be Afraid to Get a C

Some years ago I was suffering from some fairly extreme anxiety. One of the ways the anxiety manifested was that I felt like I was being constantly graded. During every meal I cooked, every parallel-parking job, every audition, every everything, I felt like someone, somewhere, was monitoring my every move and keeping track in a big notebook about how well or, more often, how poorly I was executing my life.

Exhausting.

So I decided that if I could not disabuse myself of the idea that I was being graded, then I would just try to get a C — which is the grade you get for showing up and doing the work. Not doing the work better than everyone else, not doing extra-credit work — just showing up and doing the work.

I was quite pleased with this idea, and I shared it with my sister during one of our almost-daily phone conversations. She agreed that it sounded like a jim-dandy strategy and wished me luck with it. Then we went on to discuss the real topic of our conversation that day: our father had moved into a new apartment and we wanted to send him a housewarming gift. I said I would take care of it.

A day or two later we were on the phone again and she asked me if I'd sent anything to Dad yet. "Well, no," I explained, "because I want to get him something nice but still within our budget, and I was thinking about something for his kitchen although he already has quite a bit of kitchen stuff so maybe there's a better idea if we do some sheets or maybe towels, maybe monogrammed, or —"

"Sam!" my sister interrupted. "Get a C — send a plant."

Ah, the pure ring of truth! Ten minutes later I had spent less than fifty bucks at an online flower delivery website for a handsome dieffenbachia plant, and the next day my father called both of us to say thank you and to tell us how lucky he felt to have such thoughtful daughters.

Here's the point: my desire to find the *perfect* thing for my father was preventing me from finding *anything* for my father.

My willingness to take the budget-friendly, obvious option (a houseplant) allowed me to do what we really wanted to do to begin with, which was just let our dad know that we loved him and hoped he was happy in his new digs.

How is your desire to do the perfect thing getting in the way of your doing anything?

There are two more reasons you can afford to get a C. One, your version of a C is probably everybody else's version of an A. Two, if you get your work out there and then find that it needs to be made more perfect, well, then, you'll improve it, right? That's how you roll.

I want to share a great story from the creator of WordPress, Matt Mullenweg. I'll let him tell it in his own words:

"If You're Not Embarrassed When You Ship Your First Version, You Waited Too Long"

There is a dark time in WordPress development history, a lost year. Version 2.0 was released on December 31st, 2005, and version 2.1 came out on January 22nd, 2007. Now just from the dates, you might imagine that perhaps we had some sort of rift in the open source community, that all the volunteers left or that perhaps WordPress just slowed down. In fact it was just the opposite — 2006 was a breakthrough year for WP in many ways: WP was downloaded 1.5 million times that year, and we were starting to get some high-profile blogs switching over. The growing prominence had attracted scores of new developers to the project and we were committing new functionality and fixes faster than we ever had before.

What killed us was "one more thing." We could have easily done three major releases that year if we had drawn a line in the sand, said "finished," and shipped the darn thing. The problem is that the longer it's been since your last release the more pressure and anticipation there is, so you're more likely to try to slip in just one more thing or a fix that will make a feature really shine. For some projects, this literally goes on forever....

But if you're not embarrassed when you ship your first version, you waited too long.

Confessions of a Recovering Perfectionist

Perfectionism would be so great...if only it worked.

Seriously: if you could work and work and think through every detail and really focus on achieving perfection and then have everything actually come out perfectly — that would be so great. But you can't. It doesn't work.

And you know what else would be cool? If you could achieve perfection in advance. You know — if you could think through every potential problem in advance and then start the project with the certainty that it was the perfect project. But you can't. It doesn't work.

Or what if, by hanging on to old criticisms about your past work, you could somehow make the work better? You know, someone praises you for some work you did in the past and you respond (either out loud or to yourself) by remembering every little thing that was wrong with it. If only remembering those things could somehow *undo* them, then the project could be magically revised to be perfect. But you can't. It doesn't work.

There's only one way for perfectionism to work: you have to pretend you are looking at Earth from outer space and that you can see the whole continuum of time stretched out before you. If you could have the perspective of all time and space, then you could know that your work *is* perfect. Perfect in the way babies are perfect. Perfect in the way climbing into bed after a long day is perfect. Perfect in the way pinkie toes and eggs and autumn leaves are perfect.

Defining *perfect* as "what is or what is evolving" allows every little thing on Earth to be perfect. And that is a very evolved, very loving way to view life. I really recommend it. But I find that it's tough to hang on to that perspective for more than a few moments at a time.

For years I resisted the word *perfectionist*. I thought that it sounded simplistic and anal-retentive. It reminded me of shallow, appearance-obsessed people running white gloves over lamp shades and endlessly rearranging boring long-stemmed red roses in cut-crystal vases.

Perfectionism sounded like a hobby for people who didn't have anything better to do with their time.

But at the same time, I found myself exhibiting the following behaviors:

- Endlessly thinking everything all the way through and not being able to stop.
- Not really trusting anyone else to do things properly.
- Feeling that if I couldn't succeed, I probably shouldn't try.
- Being convinced that other people were constantly judging me and my work — and often finding me coming up short (i.e., feeling I was being graded).

- Needing other people to notice and appreciate how hard I was working.
- Being unwilling to start something unless I was pretty sure I could rely on the outcome.
- Having unrealistic, if not impossible, expectations of myself.
- Having unrealistic expectations of what I could accomplish in a given period.

Now, let me point out that many of the above behaviors are exhibited by almost everyone at one time or another, and that for artists, well, "achieving the impossible" is practically our favorite pastime. Some of the greatest works of all time were the result of some artist pouring jaw-dropping amounts of money, time, energy, and life force into a project everyone else thought was totally crazy.

A Few Words in Favor of Obsession

From time to time you, like every artist, ought to have the opportunity to dive full-on into a project that consumes you. To take on a project that scares you, that requires every last little bit of your energy, your concentration, and your excellence. That pushes you and your abilities to their very limits and forces you to transcend those limits. To exhaust yourself. To go a little nuts for your art. To live, eat, breathe, and dream it. And to see what happens.

For many, that opportunity came when we were in our twenties, and it's a darn good thing, too, because that kind of single-minded energy is easier to summon (and much easier to recover from) when a body is young. But it's worth trying it again sometime. Applying the full force of your artistry to a project when you've got some years of experience behind you can be a truly revelatory experience.

Obsession has its benefits, and even the most perversely detail-oriented form of perfectionism can yield brilliant results. But, hey, not everything is a Ukrainian Easter egg, and thinking you don't want to start work because you're concerned the project might take over your life is just another form of creative self-deprivation. The middle ground is fertile ground. After all, we're looking to have a sustainable creative life.

Figuring out how to work moderately and also successfully is a problem worth solving.

Goodism

Try replacing the word *perfectionism* with *goodism*.

Goodism is about acknowledging that good can be good enough. As in, "God looked and saw that it was Good." I'm all for making things better. It's an excellent use of critical-thinking skills. It's a way to be in a state of continuous, intentional improvement. But goodism assumes that the current state of things is good, even while there is room to make them even, um, better.

But goodism knows when to stop. Unlike perfectionism, goodism just wants things to be as good as they can be. Goodism is reasonable. Goodism allows room for a good night's sleep, three square meals a day, and the ability to concentrate on other people from time to time. You know, like your spouse and your friends and your children.

Goodism also allows for other people to do their own thing without your rushing in and putting your perfectionistic fingers all over everything.

Goodism recognizes that often someone else's version of complete is done enough. Just because you would never dream of letting an un-proofread email or a sloppily formatted score out of your house doesn't mean it's wrong for someone else to. Sometimes expediency trumps tidiness. So maybe it's time for us to put away our red pen and keep our eyes on our own paper — especially when we consider the arrogance that the desire to fix other people's work implies. I've learned that I'd rather be at peace than right.

And now for the fun part. I want to share with you one of the most fun, wackadoodle, ingenious five-minute breakthrough exercise that the (amazing) Get It Done Teleclass has ever invented (so far). It is designed to help you access your intuition and your inner wisdom, and to help you think about both your project and your procrastination in a new way. Once again, there are no rules. You can't screw up this exercise. There is no right way to do it.

This exercise is also designed to be completed in less than five minutes. So take a deep breath, get centered, and allow your imagination to play for a minute or two. Work right off the top of your head. No pondering allowed.

 ## EXERCISE: THE ONE-FRAME FAIRY TALE

Start by grabbing a sheet of paper and some pens. Note: For this exercise, feel free to draw "poorly" and to use as many cheesy, clichéd fairy-tale elements as you like. If you know anything about the power of myth, you'll see that this exercise is not quite as frivolous as it seems.

The Princess

On the far right-hand side of the paper, draw an image, symbol, or word that represents your project. This image — your project — is the "princess."

Don't ponder. Whatever idea rises to your mind first is the right one. If it turns out to be not quite right later on, you can always revise it. But for now, stick with your first idea. Maybe you'll draw a book cover, or maybe it's a heart. Maybe it's an actual princess wearing a name tag that says "My Happiness." Whatever you've drawn, hooray! Good start.

The Dragon

To the left of the princess, draw the dragon that stands in the way. This is the dragon of your procrastination.

> Perhaps all the dragons in our lives are princesses who are only waiting to see us act, just once, with beauty and courage. Perhaps everything that frightens us is, in its deepest essence, something helpless that wants our love.
> — Rainer Maria Rilke, *Letters to a Young Poet*

Give the dragon a name and a shape. Maybe the dragon is a big ball of fire, or a brick wall. Maybe the dragon is a clock or a pile of clutter. Maybe it's an actual dragon. Maybe the dragon is wearing a name tag, too. Perhaps his name is "Fear of Failure" or "Can't Commit" or "What Will Everyone Think?" Whatever occurs to you first is just perfect — just sketch it out quickly, and don't evaluate.

The Hero

To the left of the dragon, in about the middle of the page or so, draw *you*. You are the hero of this story. Draw an image or word that represents you, and please have fun and be silly with this.

The Sword

Draw your weapon. This is the sword you will use to fight the dragon. Maybe it's a sword named "Good Taste" or a light saber labeled "Talent." Maybe it's a smoke screen or a bow and arrow or a pen or a camera or a flower. Allow yourself to imagine how this weapon is going to help you slay the dragon.

The Sidekick

Draw your sidekick beside or behind you. Your sidekick is the person, organization, or quality that you know you can count on, no matter what. Maybe it's a friend or partner, or maybe it's your sense of humor or your inner wisdom. Maybe it's an angel or spiritual entity, or maybe it's your MacBook. Just go with your first idea — one that makes you smile — and draw the image, word, or shape that represents your trusty sidekick on this journey.

Your Loyal Fans

Excellent — you're almost done. Somewhere else on the page, wherever you like, draw an image or word that represents me and the rest of the world's kind, supportive creative community, because I want you to know that we are with you, we are on your side, and we have your back. We believe in you. So if your faith in yourself ever falters, please borrow confidence from us. We know you can do it!

> For a free downloadable audio version of the One-Frame Fairy Tale exercise plus other complimentary resources, go to www.GetItDoneBonus.com.

You might draw us as another sidekick, or as an international army of artists marching over the hill to help you. Maybe we're the stars shining down on you, or maybe we're the sound of applause. Whatever makes you feel supported, loved, and cared for, draw that image or word.

Fabulous! You're Done! (The End)

Make whatever finishing touches you like, and then take a moment to notice what this drawing has to teach you.

- What are you taking away from this exercise?
- What surprised you?
- Did anything strike you emotionally?
- Are you inspired to take any new action based on this drawing?

- Has there been any shift in your attitude about your project or your procrastination? If so, what?

Feel free to use this exercise any time you want to get unstuck from some old thinking and show your imagination a good time.

PS: The children in your life will love creating these one-page illustrated stories, too.

There are a few other common concerns that, just like perfectionism, seem "real" but in fact are just big ol' creativity blockers. These include the voice in your head.

Who Talks You Out of Working?

Start listening to the voice in your head in a slightly different way. Start writing down what the voice says whenever you're about to embark on something new, risky, fun, or weird. Notice which thoughts actually have the power to *stop* you from doing the things you know you want to do.

You can be amazingly creative when it comes to finding reasons to quit, right?

No one cares about this.

There are already too many books (sculptures, films, poems) in the world.

Someone might steal my idea.

My third-grade teacher told me I was no good at this.

I feel like I've already tried and failed, so why try again?

I'm not good enough yet.

I haven't worked it out yet in my mind.

My work is okay, but I'm too fat/in need of a haircut/not ready.

I don't have all my ducks in a row.

What will the others think?
My family doesn't approve.

Now listen to me carefully. If you want to stand there at the pearly gates and explain to Saint Peter how you *would* have used your natural talents more except your mother disapproved and your boyfriend wasn't supportive, go ahead. But I think you're going to feel pretty silly.

The Ghosts of Failures Past

Another block to creativity are the ghosts of failures past. A client once told me, "I'm afraid to get my work out there because the last time I tried, I was sabotaged and betrayed by a group of women I had trusted." I said, "I'm so sorry that happened. That must have been excruciatingly painful. But I'm noticing that there is no group of women holding you back now. It is *you* holding you back. You are sabotaging and betraying yourself."

She launched her new business exactly seven days later.

Almost every working creative person I know has a story about the overly critical teacher, the cruel playground remark, or the scathing review that made them feel like quitting. Some of these slights were imagined, some were real, and some were richly deserved. After all, even the best artists fail from time to time. But if you let the ghosts of your failures, errors, and wrongs derail you, they will define you.

You have the power to exorcise those ghosts, but it will take determination and persistence. You must first notice when those ghosts take control, and then mentally paint them pink. Now you have hot-pink ghosts — they seem a bit lighter and sillier, yes? Good. Now call to mind a memory of one of your great successes, a time you felt valued, gifted, and good inside. Really dive into this memory and let the feeling of it suffuse your body.

Repeat this process any time those old pink ghosts threaten to keep you stuck again.

What If Someone Steals My Idea?

Sometimes the worry about someone stealing our ideas can keep us stymied. Me, I never worry about people stealing ideas. I think it's impossible for someone to steal your idea any more than they could steal your faith, your memories, or your creativity. The most they can do is copy you. Of course I encourage you to do whatever's prudent to protect your idea (registering scripts with the Writer's Guild, for example, or having collaborators sign a nondisclosure agreement, and for sure get yourself a smart lawyer), but my overall feeling is this: the best news you could ever get is that you have an idea worth copying.

Eric was furious when he found out that a colleague had copied his idea for an innovative advanced training program for healers, although he also realized that most of his anger was toward himself for not having moved forward on his own idea swiftly enough. Once he calmed down, he called his "competitor" and over lunch discovered that while there were similarities in their programs, there were also a few critical differences. Identifying those differences was an important step for Eric in developing his program, and it also gave him some terrific new tag lines and marketing ideas.

If someone copies your idea and makes a success of it, great! He's just proved your market, and now you can go ahead and do it better. (Have you noticed that there's room for more than one of something? How often two or three similarly themed books or movies come out at the same time?) And you will do it better, because it's your idea.

That said, the best way to avoid being plagiarized is contained in the phrase *speed to market*. Get your work out there first with your name on it, and you'll never have to worry about creative thievery again.

ACTION STEP

Call to mind one part of your project that is being inhibited by perfectionism, and think of at least one way in which you could get a C.

CHAPTER FIVE

How to Do Your Could-Do List

I come from a long line of list makers.

I'm a list maker, my mother is a list maker, my grandmother and great grandmother were list makers. (We're also a bunch of do-gooders, get-'er-done-ers, and eyebrow-cocking know-it-alls, but that's another book entirely.)

The nice thing about making a list is that I get the to-do chatter out of my head and onto a piece of paper. But there's no way to prioritize. There's no indication of how important anything is relative to anything else, how much time each task might take, and the order in which I ought to attack the list.

Of course, some people number their lists, but the order in which things occur to you does not necessarily reflect their order of importance. And while some people naturally prioritize, others have every item swimming around their brain in a hazy, interrelated cloud, so the list comes out all willy-nilly.

As an artist and entrepreneur, I usually have a bunch of pretty big projects going on at once, and so looking at that long, undifferentiated

There's some conventional wisdom out there that says You Should Focus on Just One Thing. To which I say: Hooey. People who like to focus on one thing should focus on one thing, and those of us who like to have lots of things going on should have lots of things going on. Although I notice that limiting my big projects to three to five at a time is often the better part of valor.

list of urgent actions makes me feel tired. Also overwhelmed and overworked — even before I've actually done anything.

Running Your Career from Your Heart

The ability to effectively prioritize your list can mean the difference between sending out another pointless mass mailing and creating a targeted campaign that yields real results.

It can mean the difference between the frustration of blindly submitting yourself for whatever projects show up on the casting website and cultivating the relationships that can get you parts that are written especially for you.

As opposed to the usual to-do list, a good *could-do* list factors in time, budget, potential return on investment, and, most important, the truth about you. Running your life and your career from your heart is the only way out of the brambles of "should-do" and into the clear sunshine of "love-to-do."

In short: a good could-do list can mean the difference between life as a frustrated, struggling artist and life as a happy, smiling, thriving artist.

Here is a story about a practical and heart-centered way to make lists, and the positive effect this system has had on my life and, subsequently, on the lives of my clients.

Vanity and Christmas Cards

One year just before Christmas, I found myself with an extremely long to-do list (you know how the holidays are), and I was having that exhausted-before-I-even-began feeling.

The first item on my list was "Make and send Christmas cards," which was something I had proudly done for years. Everybody I knew received a Christmas card with a handwritten note — always. I loved the tradition of it, I loved letting people know that I was thinking of them, and I loved the little feeling of superiority I got when I thought about how much time and care I always took at this busy time of year. I'll note that this superiority thing is not my favorite character trait, but it's important to realize how big a motivator one's vanity can be. And I was quite vain about my Christmas cards.

Adding to the pressure was the fact that I had gotten divorced that year. So not only had I moved and changed address, but also there were a number of people I felt I might "lose" in the divorce if I didn't reach out to them. Finally, I felt it was important to reassure people that even though I was no longer married to the man I had been with for nearly fifteen years, I was still me and I could still be counted on to do all the "good-girl" things I had always done. Even though I wasn't entirely sure that was true.

And Christmas cards were just one of the complicated things on my long, long, loooooong list of things that had to be done before December 25. Clearly, I needed to prioritize.

How I Prioritized the List

I took a sheet of paper, and with a big blue marker I made four columns with grid lines going across. The first column I labeled "Item/Task," and under that heading I listed all the bits and pieces of things I felt I needed to do. Every last little one I could think of. The first one was "Christmas cards," and the rest of the list filled two pages.

The next column I labeled "Time," and next to each item I estimated how much time each task might take. "Call my sister" was 10 minutes. "Finish baby gift" was about an hour. "Pay bills" got 45 minutes. If I didn't know how long something might take, I just made a wild guess or put a question mark next to it and moved on. After all, this is just a worksheet, not a government form.

"Christmas cards" got 12.5 hours. Which seems like a lot, I know, but I figured out that if I sent 150 cards and each card took five minutes to write, address, stamp, and send, then that was 750 minutes, or 12.5 hours. And that was assuming that I sent only 150 cards.

The third column I labeled "Expense," and there I listed how much money, if any, was required to complete the item. "Call my sister" got zero, since we're on the same cell phone plan. "Finish baby gift" was also a zero, because I'd already bought the supplies. "Pay bills" got $1,200, because that was about what was due. "Christmas cards" got...well, honestly, I can't remember what it got, and it wasn't a fortune, but at the time I was pretty broke and I remember it represented a significant investment for me.

The final column I labeled "Inclination." That column wasn't for facts like time or money: it was for feeling. On a scale of 1 to 10, how much did I really *feel* like doing the project? It was for the intuition-belly-check I often forgot to do. And when I neglected that intuition-belly-check, I ended up with my plate piled high with obligations to other people that left me tired and stressed out and with very little time for the things that were important to me.

"Call my sister" got a 10 — I love talking to her. "Finish baby gift" got a 7 — the little cashmere sock monkey I was making was really darling and I was excited to finish it. "Pay bills" got an 8 — I've actually never minded paying bills because I'd much rather get it taken care of than have them floating around, possibly gathering late fees and causing trouble. (I told you I was a get-'er-done-er.)

"Christmas cards." I took a deep breath. How much did I really want to send cards? Setting aside my guilt, my fear that I would lose friends, my concern that I would lose my standing as a "good girl," my sense of tradition, and my ever-lovin' vanity, how much did I *want* to do it?

I entered a 0 in the column.

That's right — I had absolutely no inclination to send even one card.

And then, in what was possibly the single most radical act of my adult life, I crossed "Christmas cards" off the list.

My little worksheet helped me to determine not only that sending cards was time-consuming and pricey but also that I just plain didn't want to. I felt strange and liberated and free, and it made me laugh. After all, any friends that I might lose because of a silly Christmas card probably weren't friends worth keeping, anyway. I had gotten the mandate from my deep inner wisdom and it said, "NO CARDS, BABY."

But, Wait...

One final word about that Christmas season. Eventually, I started to feel some twinges about a few of the people that I really did want to send cards to: my aunts and uncles, a girlhood friend, an old neighbor of mine. But I was so enraptured by my no-Christmas-cards policy that I dared not break it. See, I know me — I'd go to the store to buy just those few cards, and my resolve would crumble and I'd end up doing the whole durn thing after all.

So six weeks later, I made some lovely Valentine's Day cards and sent them off. Why? Because it wasn't expensive, it was only a little time-consuming, and I really, really wanted to do it.

(I tell this story in my Get It Done Workshop, and last year one of my clients, an artist in her midtwenties with a staunch spirit, got inspired and sent some heartfelt Valentines to some of the teachers, gallery owners, and designers she had come to know. I believe she got three separate phone calls, thanking her. Do you think those people will ever forget her? Nope. Now, that's good marketing — straight from the heart.)

Good Prioritization Can Earn You a Thousand Dollars

In time, I added one more column to my worksheet: "ROI," which stands for "Return on Investment." That's a way of determining (I just guess on a scale of 1 to 10) what, or how much, I might get back from completing an item.

For example, I had a could-do item that had been hanging around my desk for a few weeks — it was silly, really. I had found a product in a catalog that I thought a client of mine might like. I had wanted to just slip the clipping in an envelope with a quick note, but the weeks had passed and I just hadn't gotten around to it.

When I worked the list, it came up like this:

ITEM/TASK	TIME	EXPENSE	INCLINATION	ROI
Send Clipping to D.G.	2 minutes	44 cents	10	10

Wait a sec.

This was something I really wanted to do, that I thought would really pay off in the future, and that cost almost no time and no money. Duh. I got it right in the mail, and she called me three days later to book me for another ten sessions.

That little could-do item netted me more than a thousand dollars, but more than that, it helped me be the kind of person I want to be — the kind who sends thoughtful little notes to clients that I like. Again — marketing straight from the heart.

I don't use this worksheet every day, but I do use it when my list of things to do feels long, unwieldy, and confusing. Whenever I use it I discover something new, and it helps me remember why some things are important and some things, darling, just aren't.

ACTION STEP

Make a quick list of a few tasks that are on your mind, and do a "time," "expense," "inclination," and "return on investment" check for each one. What do you notice?

A Prayer for the Capable

And as you stand there
On time and
Appropriately clad for the event
With a high-fiber bar in your bag
And extra pens
Let us take this moment to applaud you.
You, the prepared.
You, the accomplished.
You, the bills-paid-on-time and the-taxes-done-in-March.
You, who always returns the shopping cart.
You, who never throws a tantrum.
While the moody, the irresponsible, the near-hysterical, and the
     rude seem to get
All the attention
Let us now praise you.
Just because everyone always expects you
To do well
Does not make it any less remarkable
That you always do so well.
So thank you.
For picking up the slack
For not imposing
For being so kind

And mannerly
And attending to all those pesky details.
Thank you for your consideration,
Your generosity,
For always remembering and never forgetting:
That a job well done is its own reward
That the opportunity to help someone else is a gift
That the complainers, the crybabies, the drama queens, the
    never-use-a-turn-signals, the forgetful, the self-involved, the
    choleric, the phlegmatic, and the your-rules-don't-apply-to-
    me-types
Need you to rebel against in order to look like rebels.
You provide the lines — for without the lines, well, what would
    they color outside of?
So take a minute
To pat yourself on the back
And say, "Job well done."
And as you consider someday
Showing up stoned
Or unprepared
Or not at all
And as you imagine someday being imperious
Or demanding
Or the one with the temper
Hear the unspoken "thank-you" from a
Grateful nation that is a
Better, smarter, calmer, easier, friendlier, and more organized
    place
Thanks to you
And your dogged diligence.
You are beautiful.
You are precious to us.

You are the hand that calms the water, the wheel that never
    squeaks, the one we all rely on
And while you probably would have remembered to send a thank-
    you note,
We forgot.
And just because everyone always expects you
To do well
Does not make it any less remarkable
That you always do so well.
And I would tell you to take the afternoon for yourself
Or sleep in tomorrow
But I'm pretty sure you already have plans.
So just take this very moment right now
To appreciate you
And all that you have done and done well
Even by your own high standards.
And remember:
You are beautiful.
And just because everyone always expects you to
Do well
Does not make it any less amazing, delightful, or delicious that
You always do so well.

CHAPTER SIX

How Many Kinds of Artist Are You?

You didn't ask to be an artist. You were born that way. And I'll bet that sometime in grade school you had a moment when it dawned on you: I Am Not Like Everybody Else.

Maybe you were moved to tears by a story or a piece of music, or maybe you were creating poetry or paintings at a level far beyond your years. Somewhere along the line, you realized that you were funnier, quicker, more adept, more visual, more kinesthetic, more manual, more verbal, more intuitive, more musical, more color sensitive, more emotional, more creative, and/or just plain *more* than the other kids in your class.

Do you remember one of those moments? Do you remember what inspired you? Take a moment now to picture that kid. Empathize with her. It wasn't easy being you while you were growing up. (Just ask your parents.) But take just a moment — right now — to say a little prayer for that sweet, inspired kid.

And while you're at it, you might want to say a little prayer for your parents and family, too. I know, I know — many of us are not exactly members of the Happy Childhood Club, but think of it from your parents' point of view: they thought they were having a regular kid, and all of a sudden they were being asked to raise a unicorn. You showed up as this very unusual child with all kinds of mysterious gifts and odd weaknesses. Honestly, I think they did the best they could under the circumstances. And I say this because in my experience everyone does the best they can under the circumstances, even if their best turns out to not be that great.

In your moment of realizing that you had all that "moreness" ("holy schmagoley — I'm an *artist!*"), you were given to understand that you looked at the world in a way that was just a little different from how all your friends looked at it.

And notice, I said just a *little* different. At the same time that you were realizing you were an artist, your friends were realizing that they had a real facility with numbers and that math made sense to them in a way that made them special. And then there were your other friends, who realized they were athletically gifted. Or the social butterflies who understood group dynamics and social politics in a way that was completely elusive to the rest of us. Or whatever it was. Every one of those kids in your class had some special skills that are just as wonderful and miraculous as being an artist.

Or, at least, almost as wonderful and miraculous as being an artist.

Remember: everyone is a creative genius in some way or other. Not everyone is artistic, but everyone's a genius.

You Are Your Verbs

Painters paint. Actors act. Writers write. Sewers sew. Latch-hook rug makers latch-hook rugs. If you are doing your verb — at any level — then you have earned the right to call yourself that noun.

Other people's approval does not make you an artist. "Getting paid for it" does not make you an artist. Good reviews, awards, publishing deals, having an agent — none of these things makes you an artist. Being famous does not make you an artist. Beginning actors are still actors. Bad writers are still writers. Unpaid sculptors are still sculptors.

So, even if you know you are still learning your craft, please —

stand tall in your verb. If you are not practicing your verb regularly, well...maybe that's something you can work on as you read this book.

But my guess is that you've got a bunch of verbs going on.

There's No Such Thing as a Single-Disciplinary Artist

I've never met a single-discipline artist. Every creative person I know says things like, "Well, I'm a writer. But I also sing in a choir and play bass guitar and drums and embroider and do needlepoint but I don't do counted cross-stitch anymore and of course everyone in my family loves to cook and did I mention that I also clog dance?"

Like I said, you're good at a lot of things. And then there's the artistry that you bring to your everyday life.

Take a look at the list of creative activities below. This list was created and then added to over the years by hundreds of students and clients. As you'll see, some of the activities on the list are a bit outside-the-box. Maybe you, too, have some skills that you never thought of as artistic?

CREATIVE ACTIVITIES

Acro-Yoga

Acting

Acupuncture

ADR (Additional Dialogue
    Recording)

Agenda Planning

All Things Mac

Alphabetizing

Animal Husbandry

Animation

Assembling Things

Awesome Salad Making

Baking

Bargain Hunting

Beadwork

Bear Hugging

Big-Picture Thinking

Biking

Bodhran (Irish Drum)
    Playing

Bomb-Diggity Smoothie
    Making
Boot Camp Sergeant-ing
Building Junk
Buying Presents
Cake Decorating
Calculated Risk Taking
Calligraphy
Camerawork
Caregiving
Cartooning
Chameleon-like Ability to
    Blend In
Choreography
Clothing Design
Coffee Making
Complimenting Others
Creative Listening
Creative Space-Making (for
    Others' Art)
Dancing: Ballet
Dancing: Boogie-Oogie-
    Oogie
Dancing: Modern
Decoupage
Detail Designing (the devil
    is in the details)
Doll Making
Doodling
Dream-Board Making
Driving in Los Angeles

Drumming
Editing
Emoting
Empathizing
Encouraging
Entrepreneurship
Event Planning
Expressing Myself Honestly
    without Being Cruel
Facebook
Fashionista-ing
Faux Painting
Film Critiquing
Filmmaking
Finding Order in Chaos
Fixing Things
Flute Playing
Foley Working
Footwear Design
Furniture Making
Gardening
Gift Wrapping
Going to the Mat
Grant Writing
Graphic Design
Guitar Playing: Electric
Guitar Playing: Folk/
    Acoustic
Gunsmithing
Handmade Card Making,
    for Prisoners

Home Cooking
Home Decorating
Honesty about Self (with Wit, Sometimes)
Horseback Riding
Idea Formation
Improvising
Information Sharing
Interior Design
Internet Marketing
Invoking
Jewelry Making
Joke Writing
Kissing
Life Coaching
Lighting Design
Listening and Giving Advice
Logistics
Long Car Trips
Lovemaking
Lucid Dreaming
Makeup application
Making Others Comfortable with Themselves
Making Fairy Houses
Marketing
Massage
Mediating
Mind-Body-Soul Coaching
Motivational Speaking

Music Producing: Stage and Studio
Needlework: Crocheting
Needlework: Embroidering
Needlework: Hand Sewing
Needlework: Knitting
Needlework: Needlepoint
Networking
Nursing
Ocarina Playing
Organizing
Painting
Painting by Number
Party Throwing
Personal Training
Philosophy
Photography
Piano: Rudimentary
Playwriting
Poetry: Limericks
Poetry of the Obscene
Poetry: Romantic
Poetry: Memorizing
Poster making
Producing
Public Speaking
Pulling Business Concepts out of My Butt (a.k.a. Entrepreneurship?)
Quad Riding
Raw Food Juicing

Reading
Reading Aloud
Reading to Oneself
Reciting
Recorder Playing
Recovery (12-Stepping)
Rollerblading
Roller-Skating
Sales
Saying No
Scabbard Making
Scenic Design
Scrapbooking
Screenwriting
Script Coverage
Sculpey-Clay Bead-Making
Set Designing
Sewing
Shopping
Show Producing: Multiple
    Genres
Shrinky-Dink Making
Silk Screening
Singing
Singing: Classical Music
Singing: Gospel
Snowboarding
Soap Making
Social Media
Software Design
Spiritual Leadership

Stand-Up Comedy
Staying in Touch
Studying/Being a Student
Stunt Fighting/Stage
    Combat
Stunts
T-Shirt Design
Talking to Animals
Teaching
Technological Geekery
Theater: Avant-Garde
Theater: Classical
Theater: Clowning
Theater: Directing
Theater: Improvisation
Theater: Industrial/
    Business
Theater: Mime
Theater: Musical Comedy
Theater: Shakespeare
Theater: Sketch Comedy
Throwing Theme Parties
Tomboyishness
Toy Making
Traveling
Tree Hugging
Tweeting
Urban Living
Vegan Baking
Video Blogging
Video Gaming

Vocals

Water Skiing

Web Design

Whitewater River Guiding

Woodcut-Print Making

Woodworking

Wrapping Presents

Writing

Writing Love Notes

Writing Meditations

Yoga

YouTube

EXERCISE: HOW MANY KINDS OF ARTIST ARE YOU?

Take a sheet of paper and divide it into two columns. In the first column, write down any of the skills or talents from the list above that you possess. Add to the list any additional skills you have mastered that you might think of as an art. Gift giving? Coffee brewing? Comforting people when they're upset? Daydreaming?

In the second column, make a note about how that talent might help you to solve a current issue in your life in a unique way. For example, remembering how good you are at throwing parties might inspire you to make your next boring meeting more festive. Calling to mind your puzzle-solving genius might suggest a fun, new way to approach your blog.

It drives me crazy when I hear an artist say, "Oh, I could never get a real job because I'm only good at one thing." Nonsense.

Spending a lifetime in the arts helps you develop all kinds of valuable skill sets: listening, reading body language, using your keen intuition; a love of history; good rhythm; the ability to present in front of a group; a sense of shape, color, and design; the ability to accept criticism; a knack for collaboration and teamwork (we usually call it "ensemble"); and most of all, the ability to think of a new idea and work hard until it's done.

I'm not saying that you have to get a real job if you don't want one. I just want you to notice how many skills and art forms you bring into every room you grace.

Once you are done noticing your own unusual art forms, you might want to take a moment to notice someone else's. People feel very seen and cared about when you take the time to praise the way they walk in the world. A heartfelt compliment such as "I notice that you are always very considered in your remarks when we have these meetings — thank you for that" can do a lot for a strained work environment. And I will tell you from experience that writing a kindly, observant thank-you note can win you a friend for life.

ACTION STEP

Select three of your special talents, and make a note about how these gifts might be useful to you in moving your project forward.

CHAPTER SEVEN

Who Are You to Do This, Anyway?

Self-doubt is a killer. It causes paralysis, night terrors, regret, and shame. And it is easily confused with genuine concerns and legitimate questions. Luckily, you can usually tell the difference the minute you state your concern out loud. Hearing your thought spoken aloud (even if no one else is around) will often make it obvious whether you're dealing with a real issue, in which case you might have that "hmm, how do I solve this problem?" feeling, or just tangled in self-doubt, in which case there's a good chance that your concern will just sound silly, even to you.

If you say your worry out loud and you're still not sure, then check with an expert. Find someone you like and respect who knows something about your area of concern, and ask her about whatever's keeping you stuck. You may find that your uncertainty is indeed well-founded and that there are steps you can take to mitigate the risk. Or she might let you know that your worry is baseless, and encourage you to go ahead. Either way, you've gotten out of your endless loop of second-guessing.

> Our doubts are traitors,
> and make us lose the good we
> oft might win,
> by fearing to attempt.
> — **William Shakespeare,**
> *Measure for Measure*

Self-doubt can also cause some other, sneakier problems as well. Let's take a look at those now.

Getting-Ready-to-Get-Ready Syndrome

The symptoms of Getting-Ready-to-Get-Ready syndrome include feeling like you can't possibly move forward until you lose ten pounds, get a degree, receive permission, know the right people, have enough money, get more experience, pay your dues, or obtain the right equipment.

The trick to defeating Getting-Ready-to-Get-Ready syndrome is doing fifteen minutes of research. (And yes, this can be one of your fifteen-minute daily tasks.) If you assume that you need to do something before you can do the thing you really want to do, please check that assumption — especially if the source of your information is your own mind. Google it, ask around, and, most important, ask someone who's already done the thing you really want to do.

Chances are good that you're overcomplicating things.

There was the photographer who was convinced she couldn't market herself until she had digitally optimized all her photos for her website, which would have meant weeks if not months of painstaking work. I asked her if she had one photo that she thought of as iconic, and when she said yes, I urged her to place just that *one* on her site. She was up and running twenty minutes later.

Lara was a highly intuitive performer who was feeling a pull toward embarking on a second career as a life coach, but she was feeling discouraged by the two years and several thousand dollars that certification would take. Now, I admire and respect the people who've gone through coach certification, but it is not a prerequisite to being of great service to people. When I pointed out that she already knew enough to at least get started with a few clients, she brightened right up. Last I heard, she was running high-end retreats once a month in Beverly Hills — further proof that if you can deliver outstanding results, nobody really cares about your credentials.

And finally, there are the countless men and women who've told me that they can't possibly get started on X, Y, or Z until they lose weight. Honey, your destiny doesn't care how much you weigh. You can find a lover, sell your art, star in your show, and earn your fortune with the body you have right now. And it's entirely possible that you will become so busy and happy working on your project that your body will self-adjust and become closer to your version of perfect. After all, there's nothing like joy to create health.

Analysis-Paralysis Syndrome

The symptoms of Analysis-Paralysis syndrome include overthinking, over-revising, and endlessly studying, often accompanied by hours of surfing the Internet. The idea that more studying leads to better answers is at best erroneous and at worst project-destroying.

Theresa couldn't stop researching website designs. Jack redid his logo fifteen times. Sharon got so involved researching her historical novel she ended up with three filing cabinets of notes and no book.

And the tricky bit about this is how very virtuous all this research often seems. Analysis paralysis seems so...rational. After all, a person wouldn't just want to plunge in willy-nilly and make stupid mistakes that could be avoided, now would she? Of course not.

So here's my offer: you are allowed to do up to eight hours of research. That's fifteen minutes a day for a month, or one straight day, or a little bit more than an hour a day for a week. Eight hours should give you plenty of information — at least enough to make a move. After all, the best lessons are going to come from your actually diving in and making your own mistakes and compassionately analyzing your successes and your failures.

Think of it this way: if you put enough good work out into the world, maybe someday someone will be researching you.

Who-Do-I-Think-I-Am-Anyway Syndrome

The symptoms of Who-Do-I-Think-I-Am-Anyway syndrome include fear of becoming too big for one's britches, not wanting to seem arrogant, and being from the Midwest. (I'm kidding. This syndrome knows no geographical boundaries.)

Who-Do-I-Think-I-Am-Anyway syndrome is a sneaky one, because it shows up at the critical moment when action is required, and it has the power to stop you dead in your tracks.

If you're like a lot of creatives, you mostly think that, all modesty aside, you're pretty good at what you do. Overall you like your work and you think others like it, too. You know you're not the best there's ever been, and sure, there's always room for improvement, but you wouldn't still be in the game if you didn't think you could win.

And then just when you start thinking, "Maybe I'm ready to submit that book proposal" or "Maybe I want a website" or "Maybe I'd like to audition," W-D-I-T-I-A-A rears it's ugly, ugly, ugly head and starts spitting out your worst fears in a chillingly logical tone.

No one cares about what you do.

It's all been done before.

Everyone and their brother is trying to do that same thing.

The world doesn't need another website/movie/one-person show/painting/novel/blog/teapot/doll/hot-pink sequin drag queen ensemble complete with feather headdress.

And then, once it's established that your work is meaningless, the voice starts in on *you*.

You're too fat.

You're not smart enough.

You don't really know anything about how to make a website/movie/one-person show/painting/novel/blog/teapot/doll/hot-pink sequin drag queen ensemble complete with feather headdress.

You don't have the right personality for this. You're too shy/
too weird/too intellectual/too depressive/too scattered/too
snobby/too goofy/too crazy/too normal/too enthusiastic/
too blasé.
You don't have the right background for this. You're too urban/
too suburban/too country/too dark/too light/too ethnic/
too white-bread/too uneducated/too educated.
You don't have the right body for this. You're too old/too
young/too tall/too short/too fat/too skinny/too sexy/too
plain/too butch/too femme/too tattooed.

Let's take one of these snarky comments, the "you're too old"
one — a real beaut, that one, and one I hear a *lot* — and examine it
a bit more.

How Could You Ever Be Too Old to Do Something?

Seriously, how could you possibly be too old? I mean, if you have an
idea to do something, then the means to carry out that idea (in some
way or other) must also be available to you, and I have never heard
of the art world putting an age cap on genius. Conventional wisdom
might put an age cap on genius, but we're not talking about conventional people doing conventional things — we're talking about *you*.

And you couldn't have done your work any sooner than now —
you were too young! I know that if you could have done your work
earlier in your life, you would have. It's as simple as that. So now
you must be the perfect age, don't you think?

So maybe you need some help (more than you're comfortable
asking for), or maybe you have physical restrictions that mean you
need to manage your energy and time in a certain way, or perhaps
you just need to direct your work to a more welcoming audience.

After years of putting her dreams of being a singer on hold,
my friend Jeanne finally started singing in public. To give herself

some experience and overcome her stage fright, she started singing in retirement communities and senior citizen centers. She said that these audiences were not only the best, most appreciative, most supportive, and most insightful crowds she'd ever encountered but also quite forthright with their opinions about how she could improve. And sure enough, one of her new fans had a son in the record business, and now Jeanne is about to issue her third CD of great American standards.

Elliott Carter was a famous American composer who twice won the Pulitzer Prize. He was extremely productive in his later years, publishing more than forty works between the ages of ninety and a hundred and more than fourteen after he turned one hundred in 2008. His last work, *Epigrams for Piano Trio*, was completed on August 13, 2012. He died on November 12, 2012, just a few weeks before he would have turned 104.

In the immortal words of advice columnist Ann Landers, when addressing a person who thought she was too old to go back to school (since it would take her four years to finish her degree), "How old will you be in four years if you don't go back to school?"

Next time you catch yourself or someone else having this I'm-too-old thought, see if you can't dig a little deeper and substitute a more accurate word.

Maybe instead of "I'm too old to do this," the truer statement is "I'm too *stubborn* to do this" or "I'm too *young at heart* to do this" or "I'm too *scared* to do this."

Another possibility is that you need to continue the sentence a bit. So maybe instead of "I'm too old to do this," the truer statement is "I'm too old to do this by myself" or "I'm too old to do this all at once" or "I'm too old to do this without prayer."

Go Ahead and Answer the Question: Who Do You Think You Are?

One answer to the question "Who do you think you are?" might be "Well, I'm the person who's going to experiment with doing this being-successful-by-working-fifteen-minutes-a-day thing."

Here is an exercise that will help you answer the question even more deeply. You can do this exercise on your own, but it's especially fun to do with someone else, since in responding out loud you are likely to be more fulsome in your response, and the other person can make notes while you talk. Recording the session isn't a bad idea, either.

 EXERCISE: YOUR HEROES

On page 86 is a table that you can fill in or copy onto a sheet of paper divided into three columns. As with all the exercises, I want you to work swiftly and right off the top of your head. No pondering. Whatever answer bubbles up for you first is the "right" one — especially when it surprises you or makes you wonder, "Why did I think of that name? That's so random!" I love those.

Step 1. Name Your Hero

The first column is a list of professions and other categories of people (such as characters and historical figures). Step 1 is to fill in the middle column with the name of someone you think of as vaguely heroic in that category. For our purposes, the word *hero* means "someone whose work you think is sort of cool, someone you'd like to have dinner with, someone who sort of tickles your fancy." Really, I mean whoever comes to mind first, even if you don't really know that much about him or her.

I have a theory that the "I can't think of anything — my mind's a blank" feeling comes over you when you're trying to think of the "right" answer or a "good" answer and that what's actually happened is your intuition/imagination has thrown up an idea or two and you've swatted them away as not being good enough or original enough. Now your intuition/imagination is standing there with her arms crossed and her eyebrows raised, saying, "Fine. You don't like my suggestions? Then *you* think of something, pal." And your mind, of course, promptly goes blank.

One client suggested I rename this exercise "Knee-Jerk Admiration," and that's a great way to think of it, because I don't want you being too strict with yourself about this list. The person doesn't have to be your *total* hero. After all, it's possible to admire someone's body of work and not admire the way he runs his personal life.

The hero you write down doesn't even have to be a famous person. It can be anyone you can think of. Heck, it doesn't even have to be a person. You may think of an animal you're fond of or a shop you particularly like. You can even write down something like "that dude in the brown sweater" or "the lady who wrote that poem I like" — after all, this list is just for you, so as long as *you* know what you mean, that's all that counts.

Take fifteen minutes right now (in truth it'll probably take you only five) and fill out the list of names of people you admire in each suggested field in the middle column of the worksheet.

Your List of Names

This list of names has some usefulness all on its own. For one thing, it's a great inspiration for Halloween costumes. It's also a great list of people to learn from, to emulate, to use as negative examples ("Oh, I'm not going to handle my finances the way *that* famous artist did!"), and to inspire you when you feel your stamina flagging.

Also, these names make terrific answers to interview questions and can

"Who do you admire? Who's your favorite author or artist?" asks the interviewer, and even though there are 1,500 books in your house, suddenly you can't think of anyone's name. Rehearse this list, and you'll never draw a blank again.

In fact, rehearse the answer to any question that you might have to answer under stress. In the words of actor and high-precision rifle smith Stephen Ramsey, "In times of stress, we revert to our level of preparation." That's why we have fire drills and dress rehearsals and why it's a good idea to practice saying how much you charge over and over again. So when the heat is on, you are sufficiently prepared and can deliver the information clearly.

spark some scintillating small talk. You can use your list of names as inspiration for a collage, a one-person show, an article, or a blog post. If you found yourself writing down the name of someone with whom you are not that familiar, well, maybe it would be fun for you to do a little research on that person. Fifteen minutes of research can yield a treasure trove of new ideas.

Step 2. List Your Heroes' Heroic Qualities

Now, going down the third column, labeled "Hero's Heroic Quality," write out what you find interesting, admirable, or fun about each person. What comes to mind? Adjectives are useful, but images can be great, too. "I love Coco Chanel because she was like rhinestones and diamonds all mixed together," or, "I love Dian Fossey because she wasn't afraid to be alone in the jungle." Whatever comes to mind first is great, and don't worry if you repeat yourself.

Do yourself a favor and be precise in the adjectives you choose. As my friend and mentor Sam Christensen points out in his insightful personal branding technology, the Image Design Process, some words in our language have become generalized and mean too many things. *Cool. Nice. Weird.* Even words like *smart* and *funny* contain a multiplicity of meanings. If you find yourself wanting to use a generalized word, Christensen suggests you go one step further and ask yourself, "In what *way* is this person X?" For example, if you put down *interesting*, you might push yourself to ask, "In what way is this person interesting?" and then you might think, "She is so interesting because she is so *innovative*." Or maybe it's a combination of attributes: "He is so interesting because he is so *pedantic* and *fun* at the same time." (Think no one could be pedantic and fun at the same time? How about Stephen Fry, or most of the cast of the current hit TV show *The Big Bang Theory*?)

MY HEROES		
HERO'S REALM	HERO'S NAME	HERO'S HEROIC QUALITY
Your own field:		
Literature/writing:		
Business:		
Fashion:		
TV character:		
Film character:		
Cartoon character:		
Music:		
Politics:		
Cooking/food:		
Ancient history:		
Modern history:		
Myth:		
Sports:		

WHAT DO YOU THINK OF AS AWESOME?

the Grand Canyon

the Northern Lights

the opening ceremonies of the 2008 Beijing Olympics

the miracle of birth

any miracle, really

These are things that are awesome. That is to say, they inspire awe.

Awe, according to my little *American Heritage Dictionary*, which I've had since the sixth grade, is "an emotion of mingled reverence, dread, and wonder. Respect tinged with fear."

So let us evaluate: a cup of coffee is not awesome. It may be fragrant, warm, desired, energizing, or delicious, but it is not awesome. Sleeping in on a Saturday is not awesome. Luxurious, sensual, restful, pleasurable, wanton...maybe. Awesome? No.

I realize my inner schoolmarm is showing, but honestly, here's this glorious word that describes a very particular kind of feeling and it has been overused and debased until now it means...nothing at all.

In his book *Skinny Legs and All*, Tom Robbins says, "The inability to correctly perceive reality is often responsible for humans' insane behavior. And every time they substitute an all-purpose, sloppy slang word for the words that would accurately describe an emotion or a situation, it lowers their reality orientations, pushes them further from shore, out onto the foggy waters of alienation and confusion."

Exactly.

Using the same word to describe a myriad of different feelings, situations, or objects is tantamount to insanity. After all, if I described everything as "leafy" you would know for sure I was crazy. "I dig that dessert, it's so leafy! And I love how leafy this restaurant is. The wine is quite leafy, don't you think? We're having such a leafy time. I just wish the waiter wasn't so leafy." "What? Only things with a lot of leaves are leafy!" you would protest. And rightly so. And only things that inspire awe are awesome.

So challenge yourself to be precise in your descriptions. The next time you feel the word *awesome* about to slip out, pause a moment and think, "What word more accurately describes how I'm feeling?" and use that word instead. After a while, you'll get good at this and enjoy your own trenchant observations.

You're probably already good at this — you're a creative genius, after all.

What words do you love? What words are you overusing?

Naming Your Attributes Out Loud

Once you're done with the My Heroes exercise, read your list of heroic qualities out loud. What do you notice? That's right. *Each one is a description of you.*

Now, you may duck your head and say, "Well, maybe that's the way I'd *like* to be...," but I'm here to tell you, honey, it's the way you are. Don't take my word for it: show that list of attributes to seven people who love you, and I guarantee that every one of them will say, "That is *so* you!"

And yes, maybe some of those words and phrases feel a bit like wishful thinking, but the seed of desire is there, and I bet you're a lot more like those words than you let yourself believe.

"But what about the bad parts of me?" I hear you cry. "What about the broken, weird, icky parts? Shouldn't I be including them, too?"

Well, I would say that we can afford to stay on the sunny side when it comes to describing you for several reasons. First of all, it's that ninety-nine delicious berries thing again. You spend so much time noticing what's wrong with you that you are missing what's right. So we need to bring your self-evaluation back into balance.

Second, you know that each and every positive quality has its attendant dark side. For example, it's great to be a "genius," but it can also be the loneliest feeling in the world. And maybe it's a blessing to be "gorgeous," but it's also a terrible burden to always be wondering if anyone can see past your face and your body, and it's tough having to adjust your worldview as your body ages.

Every adjective points to a spectrum of behaviors. We sometimes pretend that there are "good" things and "bad" things about our personalities, but if you notice, those distinctions are half-baked. Every single behavior is beneficial at times and detrimental at others.

So if you are on the spectrum of "intelligent," you have been everything from "the brilliant whiz kid who solves the problem" to an "overbearing know-it-all" — often in the same moment. And if you are "charming," you have been "fun to flirt with at parties" and you also have been thought of as "slick, oily, and untrustworthy." Am I right?

If people call you "snobby" they are noticing how "discriminating" you are. And if you are "funny" I guarantee you've been "inappropriate." And if you are "inspirational," you have also been "bossy" and even "manipulative."

Take a look at your list of adjectives on your My Heroes worksheet. When has that exact behavior caused you pain? What is the "bad" side of that behavior? When has it been your shining glory?

Embracing the full spectrum of your personality allows you to embrace the full spectrum of *you*.

HOW RAPUNZEL SAVED AN ACTRESS

Once I was working with a curvy, cheerful, dark-haired actress named Johanna who really wanted to make her mark on Hollywood but felt defeated at every turn. She was overwhelmed by the sheer number of things she could/should/ought to be doing to promote herself, and she was beating back the sinking feeling that even if she tried her hardest, her efforts would all be in vain.

The first thing I did with Johanna was the Pure Preference worksheet. It became clear that she wanted to work in film more than in any other genre. But making a movie sounded overwhelming — until we played with the scope of her project and she realized that making a three-minute film felt manageable. In fact, the more she thought about it, the more fun it sounded.

When we did the My Heroes worksheet, it came out that almost all the people on her list were women, and almost all of them were women who wielded a great deal of sexual power: Elizabeth Taylor, Jessica Rabbit, Cleopatra, and even Rapunzel. As she reviewed her list, she mentioned that she had recently had an idea for a postmodern retelling of the Rapunzel story, and maybe that could be her three-minute film project.

I love it when people make connections like this, because it proves me out: there's no right way to have a career in the arts. And I could be the most brilliant adviser in the world, but I never would have had that idea about Rapunzel — but Johanna did. Freeing herself from the idea that there was a right way to succeed in Hollywood allowed her to get to work (in fifteen-minute increments) creating the success that was just right for her.

Johanna also realized that another hidden message in the heroes list was a desire to be a little sexier in her day-to-day life — to let her inner Liz Taylor out by wearing her "really good" jeans and her kitten heels and by making sure her lipstick was on straight. "I'd like to find a boyfriend, too," she confided, "and I think that if I let myself experience the sexier, more womanly side of myself, maybe the right guy would notice me — or I would notice him!"

Last I heard, Johanna had won first place in a "micro" film festival and had three handsome men dancing on a string.

Here's another story about the Your Heroes exercise.

A BETTER LETTER

My sister is a social worker in New York City, and at the time of this story she was the head of a program at University Settlement that was a mental health initiative for children under five. If you take a moment to imagine the circumstances under which young children might need mental health services, you can imagine how difficult and stressful this job could be.

But my sister had assembled a terrific team, and when the day came for their annual office retreat (lunch and an open-air meeting in Central Park), she had her staff complete the Your Heroes exercise as one of their activities. They had a great time hearing one another's choices for heroes, and when they read their lists of adjectives to one another, well, there wasn't a dry eye at the table.

Several months later the program was discontinued due to budget shortfalls at city hall, and my sister's team decided to write letters of recommendation for one another. In composing them, they used the adjectives they'd generated using the worksheet.

I love it that these team members had so much affection and loyalty for one another that they were willing to do this, and I guarantee those letters were ten times more vivid and accurate than all those generic "this person is detail oriented and a team player" recommendations floating around. They were able to describe one another with precision and to praise each individual without exaggeration.

You might want to do a little experiment and write a letter of recommendation for yourself. Adopting the identity of a fond coworker might allow you to see some of your qualities in a new light. (This kind of exercise makes great practice for the most dreaded of tasks: having to write your own bio.)

Playing around with the idea of spectrums can also help you handle criticism. If someone calls you "fussy" and you already know you are "detail oriented," well, she's just saying what you already know, isn't she? Not everyone is going to like you, but as long as you can understand others' opinions as true in some way, you can reduce your anger and confusion at their disapproval.

Here's another tool to get comfortable with your unique combination of qualities.

Keep a List of Compliments

From now on, keep track of every compliment you get. The rule is this: only write down the phrase or adjective — don't record who said it or why or what you think she meant.

And I do mean *every* compliment. Even the ones you think don't matter, such as "Oh, you look nice today," or the generic ones such as "Good job," or even the ones that you suspect aren't really meant as compliments, such as "Oh, you are so *funny*." No matter what interpretation you might have of the words, simply write each one down verbatim:

Looks nice
Does a good job
Is funny

After you have a healthy list, review it and start noticing which spectrum each word or phrase might fall on. If there are words that really push your buttons, do a little research on them. Look them up, find out their origin, see who else has been described that way.

Sometimes the "good" stuff is harder to accept than the "negative" stuff, so you may have to do some work (start by creating some fifteen-minute art) to embrace your true fabulousness.

Here's one to start with: I think you are good and brave. (Now go write that down.)

After a short while, you will begin to notice the words and phrases that recur — those are the ones you'll want to use when asked to describe yourself and your work. (Because it's not bragging if it's true.) You may also want to refer to this list any time you start to feel disconnected from your true self: before a big meeting, a date, or a party. I've been known to sit in my car outside a party and reread my list of compliments before going in. The list reminds me that while I may feel like a big dork, in general people find me funny, kind, and helpful.

As you continue to experiment with your descriptive words and phrases, you'll find yourself becoming more practiced with them and really enjoying their subtleties. In fact, I wouldn't be surprised if the next time someone gives you a compliment you find yourself smiling that lovely smile of yours and simply saying, "Thank you."

ACTION STEP

Write down three of the nicest compliments you've ever received and post them somewhere where you'll see them regularly.

CHAPTER EIGHT

Do You Really Have to Make a Budget?

We've been discussing some of the internal causes of procrastination, but sometimes what's keeping you stuck is as simple as dollars and cents. Creative people are often notoriously disinterested in the financial aspects of their projects and consequently have a reputation for being bad with money.

My experience is more that we're just not particularly *motivated* by money; rather, we're motivated by a new challenge, by fun, by collaboration, by the joy of working. And even those of us who have a very healthy relationship with money can neglect to consider it when making our plans.

But I'm here to tell you that the word *budget* can bring great joy. Viewing your project through a financial lens can inspire freedom, creativity, insight, and new ways of thinking. This chapter contains a very easy technique to help you turn wishful daydreams into concrete reality.

What If the Money Wasn't Really the Money?

Over the years I've heard lots of old, stuck beliefs about artists and money, and sometimes those beliefs create a self-fulfilling prophecy of chronically low income and financial mismanagement. Do any of the sentences below ring a bell with you? Are there some new ones you'd add?

> *I hate dealing with money.*
> *My income is so erratic, it's impossible to plan ahead.*
> *I can't afford to save any money.*
> *Money stuff gives me a headache.*
> *People who have a lot of money are snobby.*

Now, just as an exercise, read through the above list and substitute the word *love* for the word *money*.

> *I hate dealing with love.*
> *My love is so erratic, it's impossible to plan ahead.*
> *I can't afford to save any love.*
> *Love stuff gives me a headache.*
> *People who have a lot of love are snobby.*

Now substitute the word *creativity* for the word *money*.

> *I hate dealing with creativity.*
> *My creativity is so erratic, it's impossible to plan ahead.*
> *I can't afford to save any creativity.*
> *Creativity stuff gives me a headache.*
> *People who have a lot of creativity are snobby.*

Sound silly? Good. If you can find faith in the reliable abundance of love and creativity, then you can develop faith in money, too.

Money, in and of itself, is just pieces of paper and metal. But it is pieces of paper and metal that we exchange for energy. You put your life energy into a job, and your employer compensates you with money. Someone else puts energy into a good or a service, and you trade them some money for a handbag or a sandwich or a voice lesson. Money is a means of exchange. That's it.

EXERCISE: FOUR WAYS YOU'D LIKE TO FEEL ABOUT MONEY (AND ALREADY FEEL ABOUT SOMETHING ELSE)

Make a list of four words that describe how you would like your relationship with money to be and see if you can find parallel relationships in other areas of your life. Here's a little story to explain what I mean.

MY MONEY AND I ARE MORE THAN JUST FRIENDS

When I did this exercise with Carol, a wry actress in a chronic state of just barely squeaking by, she said, "Oh, I would like my relationship with money to feel *abundant*. And totally *free*. And *steady* — I'd like to feel that money was *consistent*."

"Great," I said. "Now name another source of energy for you."

"Acting," she said promptly.

"Great," I said. "Would you describe your relationship with acting as abundant, free, steady, and consistent?"

"No," she said, laughing a little uncomfortably.

"Great," I said. "How about your relationship with your husband? Is your relationship with Jerry abundant and free and steady and consistent?"

"Yes, totally."

"Great," I said. "How about your relationships with your friends? Are they abundant, free, steady, and consistent?"

"Yes, totally."

"Great," I said. "How about your sobriety?" (Carol had been a gratefully recovering alcoholic for the past eleven years.)

"Abundant, free, steady, and very consistent these days," she said.

"Great," I said. "How about your relationship with God?"

"Abundant, free, steady, and consistent!"

"Great," I said. "How about your relationship with food? Is it abundant?"

"Yes."

"Free?"

She hesitated. "Yes."

I said, "Maybe not totally free?"

"No, not totally free. There's some bargaining that goes on with me and food. And I'm not as steady or consistent in my diet as I know I need to be."

"Great," I said. "Well done. Now we have identified some areas in which you have successfully created a healthy relationship with an energy source, and some other areas in which there's still some room for improvement. But what's important to notice is that you *can* do it. You have already done it with some things, and that means you can do it with money.

"After all, if you can keep your car clean, it's not that big a leap to assume that you could keep your house clean. If you can perform in front of ten people, it's not completely crazy to assume you could perform in front of ten thousand people. And if you can have a clear, clean, respectful relationship with one source of energy in your life, it's not too off-the-wall to acknowledge that you could have a clear, clean, respectful relationship with money."

Carol has gone on to a wildly successful career in Hollywood playing comic-relief roles in a manner that is, you guessed it: abundant, free, steady, and consistent!

But I'm Different!

But what about me? I can just hear you thinking. *My money issues are different! It's not just a question of balancing my energy or whatever it was you were doing with that Carol person!*

No. It's not. So let's have a little conversation about it.

Ack! Money is such a big deal!

Money may be a big deal, but not as big a deal as art. You can go quite some time without spending any money, but you can't go even a few minutes without needing to hear or tell a story. (Whatever your medium, all art tells a story.) And while some people can live totally off the grid and barter rather than ever buying a thing, no one can live without art. No one. When you are working on your art, you are managing a much more powerful force than mere money. Art is *infinitely* more vital than money.

But I don't understand money!

Ah, now we're getting to the heart of the matter. You *think* you don't understand money.

But I don't! I really, really don't!

Sure you do. You've been buying and selling things (including your time and talents) for years now. You know how much things cost. You know how much you have in the bank. You probably even know how much money you owe. You can make a pretty good guess at how much money your friends have, relative to you. You can probably even look at a stranger on the street and make a fairly accurate guess at how much money he has. You don't have any trouble figuring out which stores you can afford to shop in and which ones you can't. And you certainly know how much money the top artists in your field make, as well as the median and lowest amounts earned in your field. So give yourself some credit — you're practically an expert.

Okay, maybe I understand a bit about money, but I don't understand taxes and the stock market and stuff.

Darling, no one understands taxes and the stock market. And those who do make for extremely tedious dinner party guests. But let me just demystify a few things for you:

1. It's easy to keep track of your money.
2. It's easy to budget.
3. It's easy to save money for the future.

It's certainly easier to do those three things than it is to *not* do them. Seriously — taking care of your money is waaaaaaaaaay less stressful than any not taking care of your money you've been doing.

We Are Not Starving

If I could wave a magic wand and make the phrase *starving artist* disappear from the lexicon, I would. Why characterize artists as starving? We don't use the word *starving* about any other job that's unlikely to produce a high income. We don't say "starving minister" or "starving busboy" or "starving gas station employee," even though artists are, in many instances, a whole lot more likely to make a million dollars than a minister, a busboy, or the clerk at your local gas station. So, what's the story here?

People love to put artists down. "Oh, you're an actor? Which restaurant?" Ha. Ha. "You're a stand-up comedian? Say something funny." And I don't notice people in other professions getting put on the spot in quite the same way. You never hear someone say, "Oh, you're a florist? Arrange something." (We do often put doctors and lawyers on the spot, not because we want to test their right to claim their calling but because we want free advice.)

And we've all heard the sneering phrase "Any three-year-old could paint better than that. Heck, I could paint better than that." Or sing better or write better or whatever better. And maybe the person could. But she doesn't. And chances are she's never tried.

People test, deride, and sneer at art and artists as something incomprehensible and unnecessary for a reason, the same reason that bullies tease in the schoolyard: people fear what they need but don't understand. And make no mistake, people need art.

I think that one of the first things humans did that made them human was to create art: cave drawings, stories to explain the night sky, songs for hunting and for childbirth. My performance studies professor at Northwestern, the late ethnographer Dwight Conquergood, used to say that we should be called *Homo narratus* because while other animals move upright and use tools, as far as we know, none of them tell stories the way we do. (Although there seems to be increasing evidence that dolphins tell stories and that chimpanzees lie and tell jokes, so we'll see.)

We human beings are endlessly interested in other human beings. We want to see stories about them acted out on television, we want to hear jokes about them, we want to hear songs about them, we want to read books about them, we want to peer at them through windows, and we want to overhear them flirting in bars. Our appetite for information about other people is insatiable. And it is art that feeds that appetite.

No one knows why we have this capacity for self-reflection, but we do. Artists, like shamans, mystics, and priests, explain us to our-selves. So let others jeer — they may mock us, but they cannot live without us.

The impulse to squelch, to judge, to critique, and to deride art isn't going away any time soon. And hey, we ask for it, don't we? We're the ones putting our work out there at the poetry slam or the art fair or the concert hall, just inviting other people to throw rotten tomatoes at it.

Or roses. Sometimes they throw roses. And sometimes they throw money. And once that happens, no one will ever call you starving again.

There's no telling what will capture the public imagination. The great post-Impressionist painter Vincent van Gogh spent his entire tortured life penniless. In the years since his death his work has been turned into posters and key chains and calendars and T-shirts. The total net worth of all that art? A gabillion dollars.

The fact is, your art may or may not make you any money. And maybe you don't even care if it does. Creating a piece of art as a gift for a loved one or just for the sheer fun of doing it can be infinitely more joyful than working for money. Don't let anyone take away the joy you find in your work. And don't let money take away your joy.

Your World According to Money

As I've said, I'm a little tired of the myth that all artists are hopeless when it comes to money. I'm certainly tired of the myth that artists don't or can't or won't make money. In fact, every "real" job has a distinct salary ceiling. Even if you are CEO, there's still a limit to how much you'll get paid. But artists can make unlimited amounts of money, especially now that the Internet has allowed us to take the reins and distribute our own work. The fact is we do make money, sometimes quite a lot of it, and we're not really any better or worse at managing our money than anyone else.

Some artists do, however, inhibit their chances of success by keeping themselves in low-paying survival jobs and relying on sporadic, unreliable sources of income to keep themselves afloat. There are, however, a few wonderful consequences to being chronically poor. Can you think of any? Here are some that come to mind for me:

- Less stuff means less trash and less waste — you are very conservation minded.
- You almost never gamble away large sums of money.
- You are nearly impervious to advertising.
- You know how to look for a bargain.
- When the stock market crashes, you can merely shrug your shoulders.
- You know how to make something out of nothing.
- You share celebrations: potluck dinners and picnics can provide more collaborative fun than stuffy catered affairs.
- You value experiences over things.
- You know where to find fabulous cheap ethnic food.
- You see a world of possibility in every thrift store, art supply shop, and fabric store.
- You often hand-make gifts, which is lovely.
- You can see that while money can buy a lot of things, it cannot buy creative fulfillment.
- You are generally a good tipper, and you give generously to charity.

That's the good news. The bad news is that:

- You let your clothes go out of style.
- You fail to spend enough on your marketing materials.
- You are underinsured, or completely uninsured.
- You have little or no savings, retirement account, or college fund for the kids.
- You hobble yourself by using an old, unreliable computer and driving an old, unreliable car.
- You ignore important trends in the market.
- You don't take influential people to lunch.

- You keep yourself in a self-imposed ghetto of low-paying and part-time jobs that do not maximize your skills and talents.
- You are chronically exhausted from leading a financially unsustainable life.
- You don't spend enough money on self-care: massages, vitamins, vacations, preventive health care.
- You never attend expensive charity dinners or other events where people in power gather, socialize, and make friends. (Money likes to be around other money.)
- You don't charge enough, so your services are undervalued by the marketplace.

Can you see how making different choices about how you allocate your finances might affect your creative life?

Maybe you're the sort of person who lives beyond her means — buying things you can't afford because someday you'll hit the jackpot and pay off all your credit card bills.

And if you're thinking, "Well, when I'm rich I'll just have my people worry about money for me," then you are just being foolish. Rich people who abdicate responsibility for their money don't stay rich for long. You can delegate the responsibility, but you cannot abdicate it.

"Oh," you say, *"I never worry about money!"*

My experience tells me that people who say they never worry about money actually worry quite a bit about it — they just don't like to say so. And they are often so caught up in their hand-to-mouth existence that they fail to think long-term. And long-term is how the very smartest people handle their money.

> If you can't successfully manage your money when you're poor, you will not be able to successfully manage your money when you're rich.

EXERCISE: YOUR WORLD ACCORDING TO MONEY

Whatever your financial style, whether it's counting every penny or habitually throwing caution to the wind, I want you to notice something: you've created a financial system that, on some level, works for you. Which is not to say that you aren't eager to change it — I know you are. But take just a moment to answer these questions with blazing honesty:

1. How does your financial situation match how you feel about yourself and your work?
2. What family patterns around money are you perpetuating? How do those patterns serve you? How are they not helping you?
3. What's the worst thing that could happen if you changed your financial behavior?
4. What parts of yourself can you call on to handle your finances with wisdom, maturity, and fun?
5. Who is your financial hero? How can you emulate him or her in your behavior today?

Breaking the "I Can't Afford It" Pattern

Sometimes you don't move forward on your dreams because you think, "Well, I want to do this, but I don't think I can afford it, but I really want to do it, but I really don't have the money...but I want to...but I can't...but I want to...but I can't..." I'm sure you can see how getting stuck in this brain loop will cause procrastination, poor self-esteem, and that not-so-fresh feeling.

So let's bust out of this pattern by breaking things down into easier steps. Here is an exercise to help you calculate exactly how much your project will cost.

 EXERCISE: MAKING A BUDGET THAT'S FUN

This exercise will help you draw up a budget that's fun and intuitive and that gets the attention of your inner self. Get out a calculator, a piece of paper, and some colored markers (because you know this will be more fun for you if it feels like an art project).

Step 1. Make a Materials Wish List

Make a list of any materials you might want or need to execute this project. Even if your project is something fairly low-cost, such as a writing project, you may still need research materials, a new printer cartridge, a weekly trip to the coffee shop...

Think of this as a simple brainstorming experiment. You're not committing yourself to anything right now; you're just generating a list of anything and everything you might need to complete your project. If the "But I can't afford that!" voice starts piping up, just remind yourself that this is just for fun, and that part of your assignment is to write things down in the same spirit that a child might write a letter to Santa Claus.

If you don't know how much something costs, just guess. You can always double-check your numbers later on, but I don't want you getting distracted by research right now.

Step 2. List Desired Services

Next, make a list of services you might need to pay for. This might include the services of a graphic designer, a research assistant, a business coach, an editor, a transcriptionist, a babysitter to watch the kids while you work, a voice teacher, a media coach, a public relations firm, a virtual assistant, a website designer, maybe even a really good psychopharmacologist. Anyone who might help you get your project out the door should be on this list.

Again, if you don't know how much a person's services might cost, just guess. Your intuition is probably pretty close, and you can always refine your numbers later on.

Step 3. List Missed Income

Finally, make a list of any missed income this project might entail. In other words, if you're going to have new headshots taken, you might have to give up a shift at the bar, so write down the amount you are likely not to earn as a result. Or perhaps if you're pursuing the bigger-dream/bigger-ticket item of handcrafted wedding rings, you will have to turn down smaller projects. After all, the money that you would otherwise be earning (but won't be) is part of this budget, too.

Great!

Step 4. Add It Up

Now add up the totals from steps 1, 2, and 3. Voilà! Your project budget.

Are you shocked? Amazed? Delighted? Is the number much bigger or smaller than you might have imagined? Or did you pretty much know all along what the number would be?

Now is a good time to play with these numbers a bit. For example, what would happen if you multiplied your budget by ten? What if you multiplied it by a hundred? What kind of impact could your work have on the world?

Don't let yourself get hung up on the "how" or where the money would come from. You don't know that yet, and we'll get to it in a minute. For now, just let yourself revel in the depth and breadth of your project's potential.

How does it feel to think about your project this way? If you magically had all the funding you needed, how would that change the way you look, act, and think? Who would you *be* if your project were fully funded?

The Beauty of Writing Down Numbers

Another hidden advantage of writing out a budget is the clarity of seeing the actual numbers, resources, and project needs right in front of you. Even if your budget number feels huge to you, at least you know what you're looking at. If you end up with a budget of $5,000 and you currently have $100, then you know you need to start getting creative about ways to find $4,900.

Thanks to several complementary functions, your brain is especially designed to find what it's looking for. (That's why when you learn a new word you suddenly see that word everywhere or when you buy a new car you suddenly see that car everywhere — that's your brilliant pattern-seeking mind at work.)

So if you start mulling over the idea "How can $4,900 show up in my life?" I bet you'll start thinking of answers. They may or may not be answers you choose to implement, but at least you'll have some options. My friend Steph Tuss, an extraordinarily gifted business coach, sometimes recommends that a person write down thirty ways he could find the money he needs, including impractical ideas, zany ideas, and I-would-never-do-that ideas, and then picking one of the thirty and doing it. She says it's astonishing how quickly people can come up with funds when they do this process with an open mind.

Having options is infinitely preferable to being stuck in the mind loop of "I want this but I think I can't afford it...but I want this...but I think I can't afford it..." which, of course, will just cause your pattern-seeking mind to find *more* things that you want and believe you can't afford.

I have a secret belief that the action of writing down real numbers also gets the attention of your deep inner self. After all, your inner self is pretty used to you yakking on and on about things you wish you could do, but once you start writing down actual numbers, well, that's a different message entirely. "Oh! I guess we're really doing this!" says your deep inner self. "Okay, then — let's get cracking!" And you will suddenly have the support of your whole self.

Finally, there does seem to be some magic in figuring out specifically what you need and then making some movement toward it.

> When you take one concrete step toward your dreams, often the universe comes rushing in with unexpected assistance, fortuitous meetings, and plentiful support. But you've got to make the first move.

Instant Fish Tank

Some years ago I was working with a wonderful photographer in Amsterdam who, in an effort to challenge herself artistically, decided that she wanted to work with the idea of water and light. In making her budget for this project, she included the cost of a fish tank. Now, as you may or may not know, fish tanks are not exactly cheap. Particularly, I guess, in Amsterdam. But she was committed to her project and she took herself down to the aquarium shop to see what might be on offer.

No sooner did she walk in the door than she ran into a yoga friend of hers who said, "Oh, hi! Are you here to buy some fish?"

> Knowing exactly what you need allows you to find exactly what you need. Staying vague is staying stuck.

"No," replied our photographer. "I'm here to buy a fish *tank* for an experiment I'm doing with my photography."

"Ah," said the friend, "I have an empty fish tank at home that I'm not using — shall I drop it off for you this afternoon?"

Now, I can't guarantee that the minute you gain some clarity about the money and resources you need they will automatically start dropping out of the sky, but I have seen it happen quite a bit. You've probably had this experience yourself — running into the perfect person at the perfect time, or finding just what you need at a neighbor's yard sale.

> **For the free downloadable bonus article "Ten Places to Find the Money When You Think You Don't Have the Money," plus other complimentary resources, go to www.GetItDoneBonus.com.**

Now that you have your budget, you can start finding creative solutions to the unfunded elements. What expenses could wait or be pared down? Could someone you know lend you the equipment you need? Is there a down-and-dirty way to get the job done? Could you just do one part of it, say, by publishing an ebook version before you commit to printing hard copies?

Play around with your needs, and maybe ask a trusted adviser to review your budget with you. She may see alternatives or have ideas about new strategies.

ACTION STEP

Grab a piece of paper and write down the price of one thing you want but feel you can't afford. Then write down at least ten ways that sum of money could come into your life. Notice how you feel as you do this.

CHAPTER NINE

Where Will You Find the Time?

Right after "I can't afford it," "I just don't have the time" is everyone's favorite excuse for not moving forward on big projects. This chapter is dedicated to demonstrating a few new ways — really *fun* ways — to manage your schedule and make time for the work that is most important to you.

Where Does the Time Go?

There are 168 hours in a week. Or, put more accurately, there are *only* 168 hours in a week. Subtract 42 hours for 6 hours of sleep a night (I know, we're all supposed to get at least 8 hours or more, and I absolutely encourage you to do that, but most people I know with jobs and families average around 6), and we're down to 126. Subtract half an hour for preparing and eating breakfast, half an hour for lunch, and an hour for dinner, but let's assume you skip lunch at least three times a week, so that's 12.5 hours per week for eating, bringing our time to 113.5. Now, let's say you have a 40-hour-a-week job, and you spend an hour a day commuting to and from that job. You might spend 2 hours a day watching television (the average American watches a lot more — the figure from Nielsen Media Research, as of September 2012, is 4 hours and 51 minutes a day), so that's another 14 hours gone. If you go to church or temple or some other spiritual gathering, that's another hour and a half or so, and if you work out regularly, there's another 3 hours. And you need to pay bills, talk on the phone, walk the dog, play with the baby, check your email, go to a movie — so you now have 17 hours a week remaining in which to get caught in traffic, have sex, check out Facebook, grab a cup of coffee with a friend, and go grocery shopping.

So, darling, quit beating yourself up for all the work you're not doing. Finding the time for it is no joke.

On the other hand, we do manage to make time for the things that are important to us, even if it means sacrificing other things that are important to us. We sacrifice an hour of sleep to get to work early so that we can leave work early so that we can make the parent-teacher conference. We sacrifice a workout so we can have a long snuggle in bed with our loving partner. We sacrifice time to create our art so we can watch back-to-back sitcoms. And there's no judgment there — I love television. It's an important part of our culture and, as the medium matures, it's increasingly fascinating. It is also a giant time-suck.

Counting the Minutes

When we want to lose weight, we count calories. When we want to save money, we count pennies. When we want to create more time in our lives, we count minutes.

Starting this Monday, I'd like to you to keep a Time Diary for one week. At the end of each day, take a moment to look over your calendar, think back on your day, and write down approximately how many minutes you spent on the activities that made up your day.

If you're having the impulse to guesstimate, that's okay, but I think you'll find knowing *exactly* how much time you spend on each activity in your week to be tremendously useful. After all, if you want to increase the time you spend on your art, that time is going to have to come from somewhere.

One strategy is to create a Time Quilt, a color-coded table made using a sample week from your schedule. You might pick blue to shade in the time you spend at your day job, orange for exercise, yellow for religious/spiritual/self-help endeavors, pink for time with family and friends...hmm...not much open space left, is there?

Seeing your weekly schedule as a quilt will help you visualize what you are spending your time on and where you might want to make some changes.

Reverse Engineering

Another strategy is to make a daily task calendar especially for your project by reverse engineering from your goal. This allows you to break your project down into simple daily steps and can help prevent chronic everything-at-the-last-minute-itis.

Reverse engineering my calendar is one of my favorite productivity strategies. Basically, I start at the end and calculate backward. I do this for big projects as well as for my daily schedule. Let's say I want to send out invitations to a dinner party for Friday, February 22. I would want to have a final head count by the day before, so I'd put "check on RSVPs" on my calendar for the 21st. I would want to send the invitations two weeks before, so that means a note about a "trip to the post office" on the 8th, which means I need to have the invites all stamped and addressed by the 7th, which means I need to have a "get invitations printed" note on the 5th, which means I need to have the final guest list by the 29th of January. So now I know that on the 27th of January, I need to sit down and make a preliminary list of people I might want to invite, and I can schedule in some time to do that.

Making these notes in my calendar helps keep me on track and also lets me adjust for any unseen delays. I always build in a few buffer days, just in case.

For my daily schedule, I often write out my day in reverse. So, for example, if I have a meeting with Brett at 10:00 AM, my schedule for the morning might read:

10:00 AM — meet with Brett

9:50 AM — park the car

9:20 AM — drive to Brett's

9:10 AM — check driving directions and traffic

8:10 AM — shower and dress

7:45 AM — have tea and meditate

7:00 AM — wake up and take morning beach walk

And yes, I really do write it out almost every time, because the action of thinking backward often prompts other useful thoughts, such as, "Do I have the notes for our meeting in my bag?" and "Does the car need gas?"

Thinking backward through my schedule also reminds me to allow extra time for things like finding parking that can eat away at my time and, if I fail to consider, will make me late and frazzled.

One night I took a chronically late girlfriend to dinner and the theater for her birthday, and as we finished our coffee and strolled into the lobby, she remarked how refreshing it was to not to be rushing in late, having missed the opening number and feeling aggravated from caroming around the parking garage in an all-fired rush.

"Yes," I said, "I knew that if we wanted to be in our seats at 7:55 PM we'd need to be leaving the restaurant by 7:45, which means we'd need to be here by 6:30, which is why I picked you up at 5:45."

"But I was late getting dressed!" she laughed.

"I know," I said. "If I'd thought you'd be ready on time, I would have picked you up at 6:00 PM, but I figured you'd be running behind, so I allowed an extra fifteen minutes."

She looked at me as though I were a magician.

The Beauty and Magic of Deadlines

The other great benefit to building my schedule backward is that doing so necessitates the existence of a deadline. There is beauty and magic to deadlines. Deadlines inspire us to action, they set our wheels spinning, and they let us know when we're slacking off.

People often say to me, "Oh, I never get anything done until the last minute." I am here to tell you, sweetheart, that nobody gets anything done until the last minute. Now, the "last minute" is earlier for some people than it is for others — we all know people who finish their holiday shopping in August — but for those people the pressure of their internal clock makes "early" or "on time" feel like "late." Regardless, when you know what the last minute is, then you know when you need to make your move.

And if you find yourself *not* making your move, you can take a moment to analyze the reason why and take action.

Are you just plain scared? Then call a reliable friend for encouragement.

Are you lacking information? Spend fifteen minutes (only) on research.

Are you genuinely not interested? Great — perhaps you can get away with doing a half-assed job of it. (It's amazing how many things go just fine with minimal effort. Really. Try it.)

Not assigning a deadline can mean letting an idea just spin and spin inside your head, which is both demoralizing and unproductive. Setting a deadline and creating a work plan in reverse allows you to track your progress while keeping an eye on the prize.

Doing Less

This is the sort of question I get a lot:

Help me find my fifteen minutes! Life is so busy. The kids, dog, and husband need so much! I'm going crazy. Do you know how to squeeeeeeeze a few more hours out of a day?

Here is my not-kidding answer to clients who ask me these things: *Do less stuff.* That's right. You heard me. Do less. Here is a three-step exercise to show you just how to do that.

 EXERCISE: DOES IT HAVE TO BE YOU?

1. Write down all the activities that you typically do in a day, such as:

   drive in the car pool
   do laundry
   pay bills
   make phone calls
   write
   work out
   get the mail
   read
   work with clients
   play with the kids
   plan upcoming travel
   coordinate volunteers for charity event
   go to the grocery store
   cook supper
   watch TV

2. Now put an asterisk next to the tasks that only you can do. So the asterisked items might be:

   write
   work out
   read
   work with clients
   play with the kids

3. Find a way to get the unstarred items off your plate. You may need to hire someone, or you may need to simply ask some of the other grown-ups in your life for help. Teach the kids to do the laundry, and get a cochair to work with the volunteers. Yes, you will have to get over some of your perfectionism — nobody else is going to do as good a job cooking dinner or sorting the laundry as you do. But guess what? You have bigger fish to fry.

> The work that only you can do, you must do. The work that anyone can do, someone else must do.

Your creative life is never going to take precedence over your everyday life unless you make it happen.

How to Say No

I've had so many clients tell me, "People ask me to do things...and I just can't say no." Of course people ask you to do things. You're good at stuff, remember? And if you're like many creatives, you may not keep much of a regular schedule, so people think you have all kinds of free time.

But I understand not wanting to say no. I'm that way, too — if you corner me and ask me to do something, I'll automatically just say yes.

In fact, many years ago I was in therapy, and during one particular session I was talking about a play I'd been asked to be a part of. It wasn't normally the kind of show I would jump up to do, but I was flattered because they had asked me — I didn't have to audition, they were just inviting me to be a part of it — and I knew from experience that once involved I would probably have a good time. I was nattering on in this vein, about how I wasn't sure even though it would probably be good for me to do it, and I was pretty sure I could make it work with my already-overloaded schedule and —

"Sam," my therapist interrupted me, "can I tell you something about you?"

"Sure," I said.

"When you want to do something, it's done. You don't hesitate, you just do it, and usually in record time. When you *don't* want to do something? You equivocate."

Man, did he earn his $25 co-pay that day.

More than once in my life I had waited to hear the big "no" buzzer go off inside me. Turns out, I don't have a big "no" buzzer. I have a buzzer that says, "Well...it could probably work...I think I could do it...and I'm sure it would be fine..."

That kind of waffling is my version of no.

So now I listen to myself very carefully, and I've instructed my friends and coworkers to listen, too. If I am equivocating at all, that means no. After all, just because a person can make something work doesn't mean she should.

It also helps to allow time to check in with yourself before answering. Whenever someone asks me to do something, I now automatically say, "Thank you so much for inviting me to do this thing. Let me consult my calendar, and I'll get back to you later today (or after the weekend, or whatever)." Then I really do check my calendar, as well as my finances, my intuition, and my inclination meter. If all systems are go, then, great — I call back and say yes.

But if the answer is no, then I call the person back and say, "Thank you again for asking me. I'm afraid I'm just not available for that right now."

And you know what? No one ever gives me a hard time about it. Never — because they know I thought about it. Sometimes, if you say no right off the bat, people will argue with you and say, "Oh, please — it'll be really fun and so-and-so will be there, and it just won't be the same without you," and you'll relent. But if you take some time to think about it and then say no, people feel as though their request has been honored. You can also add something like, "Please ask me again next time, though, okay?" and they'll be tickled pink (but only say this if you really would like to be asked again).

In this way, you honor the request, you are respectful of the person asking you, and you honor yourself. Pretty good trick, hmm?

Teach People Your Schedule

"Arghhh!" said Julie. "My clients are driving me insane! They are constantly calling me, asking me questions, wanting this thing or that. And I always get back to them right away, but if, heaven forfend, I try to take an hour for myself they totally freak out. 'Why aren't you answering your phone?' they say. They have no respect for my time!' I even had a client call me at eight o'clock on a Sunday morning because she wanted to change the background color for her flyer. I mean, seriously, who raised these people?"

"Did you answer the phone when she called at eight on a Sunday morning?" I asked.

"Well, of course," said Julie, "she's a client."

"Then you raised her," I said. "You have taught her that you are available at all hours and that you always respond right away."

"Oh. Oops," said Julie.

It's never too late to educate people on how to treat you. But just as with training a puppy, you must be firm and consistent. No slipping treats under the table in the form of late-night texts or doing last-minute revisions for free. You must reward positive behavior and ignore the negative.

Here are my rules — please feel free to crib from them:

1. On my outgoing phone message I explain that I return calls within twenty-four business hours, so if you call me at

5:00 PM on a Friday, you may not hear from me until Monday afternoon.

2. I return emails within twenty-four business hours, too, and so sometimes I will compose an email but wait to send it until the next morning, just so that people don't start expecting me to always reply right away.

3. Unless I am both available and in the mood, I let most calls go to voice mail.

4. I don't allow electronics in the bedroom.

5. I usually don't touch the computer on Sundays.

You also need to be firm about your boundaries in other ways. It is not rude to be firm about your agreements; it is respectful. Consider adding these rules to your life:

1. Always start all meetings, workshops, and sessions on time. Do not go over time without the permission of the group.

2. If you notice "scope creep" (someone asks you do something fairly simple and then, over time, starts adding other little bits and pieces until it has actually turned into quite a big job), you must stop work immediately and have a conversation with the person about exactly what he wants done and how much more it's going to cost him.

3. When it comes to deadlines, always underpromise and overdeliver. You're much better off telling a client the job will be done on Thursday and finishing it on Wednesday than the other way around.

4. Build in penalties for clients. If a client is late, she forfeits that part of the session. If she cancels with insufficient notice or doesn't show up at all, she will be billed in full. If she fails to provide the materials you need to move forward, there is a financial penalty. The idea here is not to be a policeperson but, rather, to block out time, make decisions, and keep yourself available to do work for your client. If she doesn't

show up or doesn't provide you with the proper materials in a timely manner, well, too bad. She has bought your time, attention, knowledge, and availability. She is not doing you a favor by providing you with work. You are engaged in an equal exchange of money and skills, and you are partners in getting the work done. It's okay if your clients are a little afraid of you. After all, you have talents they know not of.

5. In turn, make sure you are respectful of other people's time. Be prompt for your haircut appointments, dinner reservations, and child's piano recital. I even like to arrive places early — it's amazing how much good thinking you can get done while you're just sitting in the car for ten minutes.

Now, if all this starts making you feel like you might break out in hives, don't worry. Chronically late people can be successful, too. Just make sure you alert everyone to your rather, ahem, *elastic* sense of time, and if you can, hire a right-hand person to try to stay on top of things for you.

ACTION STEP

Remove one thing from your schedule. Permanently.

An Ode to the Overwhelmed

And as you stand there
Late again
Because you forgot to allow time to park
And the elevator was slow
And you left ten minutes late to begin with
With your shoes that pinch
And your pants that are a little too small
Since you started eating white bread again
And as you paw through your bag
Looking for the suite number
That you're not sure you wrote down to begin with
Let us now praise you.
You, the untidy.
You, the careless.
You, the easily distracted by sparkly things.
The money you spend on late fees alone
Could feed a family in Africa —
Which reminds you that you meant to send in the kids' UNICEF
    money and
Forgot
But you are good and brave.
You, flying by the seat of your pants
Making it work

Putting out fires

Saying your prayers

And dancing your dance of now and later and maybe and

I'll-have-to-call-you-back-on-that-could-you-send-me-an-email-
to-remind-me-to-call-you-back-on-that?

As innocent as each morning's sunrise,

You are a fount of good intentions.

Your good humor is as graceful as a baby giraffe,

Even if that joke you were trying to make to the hotel clerk fell
flat

And your toast at the wedding came out sounding a little...funny.

But you have gifts that no one knows about.

You have the strength to bend in the wind

You have the joyful spirit that loves a good belly laugh,

You have the wisdom to understand that everything will all come
out all right in the end and

You have the faith to light a candle rather than curse the darkness.

(That is, if you could find the book of matches from that romantic
restaurant you went to for your anniversary but since you
didn't have a reservation they made you wait at the bar for
half an hour during which you had two appletinis and the rest
of the night is a bit of a blur.

So much for the overpriced lingerie.)

You are beautiful.

Frazzled and overworked and underpaid

You are the one who forgot your wallet

And forgot your receipt for the dry cleaner's

And forgot your keys, which you just set down five seconds ago,
so where could they possibly have gone?

But you never forget to say, "I love you"

And you never forget to give a big smile to that nice parking guy

And you never fail to show endless patience when the

Too tightly wrapped and overly conscientious start to offer their
Oh-so-helpful suggestions about how you might feel better if you
    would just learn to alphabetize your spice rack.
You are beautiful.
So, wear the lingerie on Monday for no reason.
And why not just refuse to participate in the bake sale this year?
And give yourself a compliment for something you did well
    today.
Because you are the most beautiful woman I've ever known.

CHAPTER TEN

Organizing Your Space

I don't believe that it's all that important to be organized in the way the magazines always make "organized" look. I mean, if you use your space, it's going to get messy — probably almost every day. And that's okay — messes can be a sign of life, activity, and creativity.

So quit beating yourself up that your place is not all perfect-schmerfect. Instead, think about what's working for you in your space and what's not working for you. If you're spending a lot of time looking for things you've misplaced, that's not working for you. If you're losing track of bills and important papers, that's not working for you. If you can't really clean your space because there's stuff piled everywhere, that's not working for you. Those are all examples of systems that aren't working for you.

> Elegant systems have beauty, simplicity, and grace. They are easy to explain and easy to use. They bring peace and, perhaps surprisingly, create space for increased spontaneity and joy.

Good Systems, Bad Systems

Now think of some systems that *are* working for you. Give it a minute, because often we don't think about or notice our good systems. For example, you have a system for getting your car out of a tight parking space, but you never think about it. That's the beauty of a good system — it removes the need for us to think about every last thing all the time and frees up our minds to think about more interesting things. Like our art.

Here are some examples of good systems:

- The minute she picks up the photos from the developer, Sasha writes the date and a short description on the outside of the envelope. "Graduation, June 2013." "Vermont Vacation, October 2011." Then she places the envelopes in chronological order in a photo box that lives on the bottom shelf of the bookcase in the living room, because her young daughter likes to look through them. "Real photo albums are just too much pressure," confesses Sasha. "I used to feel bad about it, and I'd buy the albums and scrapbooking stuff but the photos would just pile up — taunting me." She laughed. "So now I have a system that may not be as pretty, but it works!"

- When Thomas gets a bill in the mail, he opens it immediately — and I mean even before he takes off his coat — and checks the due date. Then he writes the date that the bill needs to paid by (usually ten days before the due date if he's mailing it in and four days before if he's paying online) on the outside of the envelope. So on a phone bill that's due by August 14 he writes "8/4" on the envelope. Thomas then puts that envelope in a little clear holder on his desk with all the other bills stacked in order of their due dates. All Thomas has to do is glance at that holder to know when he next needs to pay bills. "It only takes half a minute when I walk in the door each night, and I'm a much more relaxed daddy knowing that there aren't any unopened surprise time bombs sitting around."

- Stephanie loves her magazines, and she keeps them in a basket next to the couch so they're close at hand whenever she wants to read. When the basket gets full, she throws a few of the older magazines into the recycling pile.

Human beings systematize everything. We can't help it.

You have a system for doing the dishes, you have a system for paying the bills, you have a system for determining which television show you're going to watch, and you have a system for keeping track of your stuff. It may not be a very good system, but it's a system.

Throwing wet towels on the bathroom floor when you're done drying off is a system. It's a flawed system, but it's a system. And it's not flawed because it's messy. It's flawed because the next morning when you get out of the shower, all you have is a wet, crumpled-up towel when what you want is a nice dry towel. The system is flawed because it doesn't solve the drying-off problem.

The first step in creating a good system is to think about the whole problem. And rather than use the word *problem* let's instead think about what we want. What is your *desire?* In this case, the desire is simple: I want to dry off with a dry towel every morning. And there are a lot of ways I could satisfy that desire:

- I could buy a new towel every day.
- I could buy seven towels and stack them near the shower, put a plastic-lined laundry bin next to the tub, and then commit to doing the wash once a week.
- I could install a dryer near the shower and immediately put damp towels in to tumble dry.
- I could spread the wet towel out over the towel bar so that by the next morning it would be dry.

Some of these solutions may seem impractical, but that doesn't mean they wouldn't work for somebody. Let's look at our examples of good systems again, and name a few of the elements that make them good:

- All the systems are timely — they only take a few seconds, and they are immediate. In other words, the photos/bills/

old magazines don't clutter up the dining room table while someone figures out what to do with them.

- All the systems involve creating a "home" for something. The photos live in the box, the bills live in the holder, the magazines live in the basket. The home is the right size and is in the right place.
- All the systems eliminate the need for thinking. In other words, by labeling something with a title ("Vermont Vacation, October 2011") or a due date ("8/4"), we can tell at a glance what it is. We don't need to pick up, examine, and evaluate it every time. Stephanie doesn't need to waste time wondering if it's time to get rid of some magazines. She knows it's time to get rid of magazines whenever her basket is full. It's a no-brainer.

> Give me the discipline to get rid of the stuff that's not important, the freedom to savor the stuff that gives me joy, and the patience not to worry about the stuff that's messy but not hurting anybody.
> — Vinita Hampton Wright, *Simple Acts of Moving Forward: A Little Book about Getting Unstuck*

It's time for you to figure out which of your systems are working for you and why. To that end, take a crack at answering these three questions:

1. What are three of your good systems?
2. What makes them good? Why do they work?
3. What do these systems have in common?

Now think about the space in your life that you think needs work, and complete this statement: I want my space to feel _____ so that I can _____.

"Clutter clearing," "getting organized," and "getting my sh*t together" are all examples of really bad project names that are discouraging and uninspiring. Unearthing the "why" of why you want to clear your clutter gives you a much better project name and a much more inspiring goal.

See, now we're not just "getting organized"; we're creating a space that, for example, feels "open and friendly" so that we can "invite friends over spontaneously." Tying the work of clearing out and organizing to your dreams and values will motivate you to action and will help prevent backsliding.

Now Find the Time

Organizing takes time. So do yourself a favor and don't start until you have enough time to finish. Either that, or tackle the job in little bits — don't do the whole closet, just organize the shoes.

I have a friend named Erin who clutter-cleared her entire house in five-minute increments. At the time she was working from home and had two very robust toddler boys, so finding a whole fifteen minutes felt like a stretch. "But five minutes, I could do," she reported. "I used the timer and everything. I labeled the timer 'Wide Open Spaces,' and once or twice a day I would set it and just do, say, part of the silverware drawer. Or fifteen inches of bookshelf. The boys got into it, too — it was a fun game for them and we still do it all the time. It took me about eight months, but by the end, the whole house looked like a picture out of a magazine. My mother couldn't believe it when she came to visit. That felt *really* good."

Another good strategy is to invite someone over to keep you company while you, say, empty out your guest room closet. Let me be clear: you are not asking her to help you clean out your closet; you are asking her to sit with you and have a glass of something while you do the work. This is an effective strategy for two reasons. One, if you know someone is coming over, you will keep the time clear and not let yourself get distracted by other things. Two, if you know someone is coming over, you will often do a lot of the work ahead of time, because you're too embarrassed to let this person see your space in its present condition.

That's fine. Vanity is a perfectly good motivator. I myself am not above scheduling a dinner party just so I can get around to deep-cleaning the carpets. Bribery is good, too. So is outsourcing — there is no shame in paying someone else to do whatever needs to be done. When it comes to cleaning and clearing, I say: Do whatever works, honey.

Now it's time to get rid of some stuff.

Don't panic — I didn't say, "Get rid of everything." I said, "Get rid of some stuff." Take a deep breath. Take frequent breaks. Don't forget to eat something. If at any time in the process you feel wobbly, get a drink of water, remind yourself of your dreams and values (e.g., "having an open and friendly space so you can invite friends over spontaneously"), and keep going. Even doing a little is better than nothing.

A Few More Suggestions for How to Get Rid of Things

Here are few more ideas that have worked really well for clients — and for me.

What If You Needed $50,000 Right Away?

Play along with me for a moment: What if you needed to raise $50,000 right away and the only way to do it was by selling off the things you own? (If you want, you can pretend you're in an old-fashioned TV movie and there's an orphaned child who needs an operation or something.) Here's a brief exercise to get you in the spirit:

 EXERCISE: IS THERE MONEY HIDING IN YOUR HOUSE?

Make a list of ten things you would sell and how much you think you might get for them. As usual, work as swiftly as you can, and don't be afraid of writing down whatever comes to mind. After all, you're not actually going to sell these things — this is just an exercise.

How do you feel about your list? Are you surprised by what you wrote down? Has writing this list altered how you feel about any of these objects?

One of my clients who did this exercise, Eva, reported that the first thing on her list was to sell the family china. She was amazed at how willing she was to get rid of her grandmother's china service. "I always thought I had to hang on to it, because, you know, she was my grandmother and the china is frightfully expensive and really beautiful. It's so beautiful and expensive that we never use it. But once I thought about it in terms of 'saving a life,' it was obvious that it's just a bunch of plates in a box in the basement that aren't doing anyone any good."

Eventually, Eva consulted with her husband and sisters, and they decided to sell the china and use the money to help fund their first-ever family reunion. "This exercise helped me realize that the true legacy of my grandmother was the family she created and nurtured. In the long run, the plates weren't important, but the people gathered around the table were."

What did you discover? Might you be willing to part with the jewelry your first husband gave you? The skis that haven't seen a slope in five years? The handmade dollhouse that no one's played with since forever?

If you are living in an overly cluttered space, then, if you'll forgive the metaphor, the "orphaned child" in this movie is your life — struggling to breathe amid all this suffocating stuff.

Location, Location, Location

If you get dressed in the bedroom but your jewelry lives in the bathroom, that's not working for you. If you like being in the center of the action but your desk is in the attic, that's not working for you.

If you need privacy but your easel is in the playroom, that's not working for you. Notice where you are actually doing your work. Here are a few stories about clients who created a bit more congruency in their lives.

THE COUCH AND THE CLOSET

Peter is a sweet-tempered screenwriter with a tendency toward pessimism. He usually works on his scripts while seated in a corner of his big couch in his living room. As a consequence, his coffee table is covered with papers and CDs, and there's usually a pile of source material, old copies of *Variety*, and various notepads stacked by his feet on the floor.

When I suggested that a medium-sized bookcase and a good lamp next to his couch might make the place more orderly, Peter demurred. "I should really work at a desk. I'll just move all this stuff to the desk."

But I would not be put off. "Peter, I notice that there are two desks plus a dining room table in this apartment, and clearly you are not using any of them. You *like* to work here on the couch, so let's make your work spot work for you!"

One bookshelf, one floor lamp, and three CD storage cases later, Peter was happily typing away. He sold both of the desks — and his latest screenplay.

Meredith loves to multitask and to be in the center of the action. As a writer who specializes in articles, essays, and short stories about children and family life, she found her little office in the upstairs bedroom isolating and ineffective. It seemed like no sooner did she sit down, than one of the kids needed something, or she wanted a cup of coffee, or it was time to make dinner.

Or maybe she just felt like those things *might* happen and she would miss them if she were trapped upstairs. So she turned the upstairs room into a much-desired retreat for her eldest child and moved her desk to a little nook just off the kitchen. She moved her files into the front hall closet (which, I must add, only works because Meredith lives in Southern California and so she doesn't really need her front closet for coats) and turned the closet doors into a bulletin board. Now she loves typing merrily away while the pasta water comes to a boil and her husband watches TV. Frequent interruptions wouldn't work for everyone, but Meredith finds that being in the midst of domestic chaos cultivates her creativity.

Nontraditional work spaces can work perfectly, if they truly accommodate your needs.

Getting Organized: The Kitchen, for Example

It's pretty obvious that the way one artist needs to organize a loom and hand-dyed wool is different from the way another artist needs to organize Sculpey clay and jewelry-making supplies is different from the blacksmith's way is different from the knitter's way is different from the jazz singer's way.

And the way each individual jazz singer needs to organize her materials is different from the way her fellow singers need to.

Therefore I'm going to give you a few tips on organizing based on the one thing we all have: a kitchen. You may or may not use yours, but I love mine, and I love cooking. My kitchen is very tiny (perhaps your work space is tiny, too), and it gets used all the time to create unique dishes full of love. So think of my kitchen as a metaphor for your space, and see how many of the lessons you can translate to make your space work better for you.

Single-Use Items Not Allowed

I don't believe in bread makers, sandwich grillers, rice cookers, or pasta machines. If homemade bread or grilled sandwiches or rice or fresh pasta were more of a staple in our diet, I might reconsider, but as it is, no single-use items are allowed in my kitchen, especially if they are big and bulky. To sacrifice precious cabinet space to a bread maker that will see the light of day exactly twice a year is, I think, a big waste. I'd rather have a food processor that can chop, slice, blend, *and* knead.

Of course, some single-use items are essential. Only a corkscrew can open a wine bottle, and it doesn't do anything else. Which is why, in my book, one small, plain corkscrew is okay and those giant, expensive corkscrews aren't. No giving over space to anything large that does only one thing!

My friends think this is hysterical and have a lot of fun trying to stump me, but it's not as if I've got hard-and-fast rules. The decision about whether to have something depends entirely on your preferences. "What about coffeemakers?" my friends say. If you drink a lot of coffee, then great, sure, of course, have a great coffeemaker. I don't drink a lot of coffee, so I have one of those very low-tech stove-top Italian espresso makers that is quite unobtrusive and makes one heckuva cup of joe.

"What about electric teakettles?" See, I drink a fair amount of tea, and a pot on the stove has always worked just fine for me. I don't even use a regular teakettle. But if you're in an office or someplace where an open flame would be unadvisable, then sure, have an electric teakettle.

"Spice grinders? Fish scalers? Melon ballers?" Again — if you find yourself grinding a lot of spice, scaling a lot of fish, or balling a lot of melons, then, great, go get yourself what you need. If not, then don't.

Tools are fun. Clutter is not. When in doubt: choose fun.

Find It Where It's Supposed to Be

I alphabetize my spices. Again, my friends laugh at me, but I don't mind. Ask me if I have any cumin. Go ahead — just ask. I can answer you in about a second. And when I'm putting together a recipe or making a grocery list, I love knowing exactly what I have and don't have.

Is your essential equipment organized in such a way that you can tell at a glance what you have?

I organize the shelves in my refrigerator, too, putting like with like: pickles, relishes, and salsas in one row; sour cream, yogurts, and cottage cheese in another. All the jams and jellies live on one shelf, all the salad dressings on another. My husband's collection of olives lives on yet another shelf on the door. (Why do we have a collection of olives? I don't know. You'd have to ask my husband. But if we ever run out of olives, we'll know about it.)

Anything that might spoil goes front and center. (See "Frequency of Use" below.) That's why I put fresh veggies on the middle shelf and use that silly crisper drawer for sparkling water and soda pop. If I put vegetables in that drawer, I guarantee I will forget they are there and they will go bad. If I put vegetables right in the middle where I see them every time I open the door, I will remember they are there and I will cook them for dinner. Yum.

Some people think organization inhibits creativity. I am here to tell you that *organization is the key to creativity.* Knowing what you have and being able to access it easily encourages flow, encourages use, and encourages courage. So — dare to be organized!

Frequency of Use

I hate having to fumble around with my pastry brushes (which I use maybe once every three months) while trying to get to my kitchen shears (which I use at least twice a day). So I moved my pastry brushes and my cheesecloth and my rolling pin and my nutcracker and my mandoline to a bin in one of the lower cabinets. The bin is labeled "Seldom-Used Items" and now the frequently used kitchen drawer is clean and clear. My kitchen shears are right where I want them, every single time.

I arranged my pantry cupboards the same way: staples and snacks are on the lower shelves, exotic ingredients and specialty foods are up high. After all, why should I waste time shoving aside the nori and the nutritional yeast when all I want is a can of black beans?

Keep your current materials close at hand and the things you use most in easy reach. Put the specialty items that you rarely need farther up — or perhaps you can get rid of them altogether.

Only One Junk Drawer Allowed

Every kitchen is allowed one junk drawer in which to store all those weird miscellaneous items that just don't seem to belong anywhere else. Should your junk drawer spill over into two junk drawers, then, darling, you have too much junk.

Sift through your items and see what can get thrown out (probably quite a bit) and what could live somewhere else. Again, put like things with like: my rubber bands and those plastic tabs you use to close the bread bag used to clutter up the junk drawer, but now they are all in a tiny square cup tucked in with the plastic wrap, aluminum foil, and Baggies.

If you find yourself going into your junk drawer frequently, then it's probably not really a junk drawer. It probably has a secret identity. Your junk drawer might actually be a tape and kid-friendly scissors drawer that also contains drinking straws, half-used birthday candles, and the menu from the Chinese place that delivers. So make it a "Kid-Friendly Office Drawer." Lose the old candles, move the straws, and create a file folder for take-out menus that can live with the cookbooks. Then add in some washable markers, rulers, scratch paper, and stickers. Fun, right?

Where Will I Think to Look for This Later?

Asking yourself the question "Where will I think to look for this?" might be the single greatest organizational step you can take. Asking yourself this question puts you in a state of awareness about your organizational style and creates an automatic mnemonic so you are even more likely to remember later on.

If I can imagine that the last time I put away a bottle of vanilla extract I thought, "Well, I'll probably think to look for this with the rest of the baking stuff or maybe with the spices," and then I put it with the rest of the baking stuff, well, I've got a better than fifty-fifty chance of finding it right away the next time I need vanilla. Certainly much higher than if I just jam it on a shelf somewhere where it eventually gets shoved to the back (because it's a seldom-used item) and where I'll never find it because I'm not even sure I have any to begin with because I don't remember the last time I put it away. This leads to buying more vanilla extract, which, if you use

What are you not using? Some power tools or sewing machines or paper-making tools are fabulous, useful items. Some are not. Some you rarely use. Some take up too much space in relationship to their usefulness. And some seemed like such a good idea but turned out to be just giant dust catchers. Let them go. You need the space, and you don't need the guilt of having a big appliance that you don't use.

You may also want to send out some feelers about who might have something that they are willing to share. Often places with big machinery are happy to rent to you by the hour; it offsets their overhead and allows them to give back. Community centers, colleges, and even businesses can be terrific resources for things like large-scale printing, metal-working, and high-volume work.

the pure extract (and you really should; the imitation stuff is terrible) is pretty darn expensive.

So why buy two when one, well placed, will do?

Again, the question is not, "Where *should* this go?" because that leads to unhelpful thoughts such as the kind Peter had about the desks he never used. The question is, "Where, given my actual life, would I think something like this might end up?" This is also a great question to ask yourself in parking garages, although there it sounds more like, "How will I remember which spot this is when I return?"

A good system is practical, realistic, easy, and even fun.

A bad system is impractical, unrealistic, hard, and a bummer.

You, your stuff, your space, and your art all deserve great systems.

Do I Use It? Do I Love It?

Here's the simplest way to sift through your belongings. Ask yourself, "Do I use it? Do I love it?" If you love it, then keep it. If you don't, out it goes. End of story.

It is okay to keep something you love. You don't need to explain it or defend why you love it. But it does need to be True Love. That is, it must make your heart swell. It must make you feel good.

Feelings of nostalgia, guilt, sadness, sentimentality, shame, fear, anxiety, or depression are not the same as the feeling of love. Be honest. Be remorseless. This clutter has already cost you plenty in space, time, and unease. You deserve to have things around you that you love. And you deserve to let go of the things you don't love — to make room for more love, of course!

Now, answering the question "Do I use it?" is generally pretty easy. The stuff you use, you keep. The tricky part comes when the answer is "No, I don't use it, but..." These *but* thoughts are what stand between you and a clean, inviting, organized space.

But I might need it sometime.
But if it were fixed I would use it.

But if I fit into it I would wear it.

But it's so nice.

But it was so expensive.

But it was such a great deal.

But my mother gave it to me.

But I could sell it on the Internet or at a yard sale.

But it reminds me of that special time.

But it's a family treasure — I want to keep it for my children and my children's children.

The *buts* are endless. Enlist a friend or, better yet, a professional to help you be honest with yourself and move through these self-imposed limitations.

If you prefer to do this work alone, let me provide a few challenges to your *buts*.

But I might need it sometime. If you haven't needed it up to now, the chances that you'll need it in the future are pretty slim. And if you do need it in the future, I bet you'll be able to find an even better one easily and inexpensively. The universe is both great and abundant, and you are remarkably resourceful. Have a little faith, okay?

But if it were fixed I would use it. But you haven't fixed it yet, and you've lived without it working for *how* long? Seriously, hanging on to broken things is bad mojo. If you really, really, really want to fix it, then take it out to your car and put it in the front seat right now. The next place you go is the repair shop. Or the frame shop or the tailor or wherever. If it's worth hanging on to, then it's worth being fixed promptly and treated with respect.

But if I fit into it I would wear it. There is a big myth that hanging on to clothes that are too small for you is a good incentive to lose weight. Guess what — it's not. It doesn't work. If it worked, you would fit into those clothes. What is not a big myth is that having a closet full of clothes that fit and feel great will elevate your self-esteem and help you achieve the body you want. Let the small (or big) sizes go — someone else needs these clothes while they're still in style. And when you do reach your ideal weight, you will be able to find fabulous, *current* fashions that delight you. I promise.

But it's so nice! Yes. It's very nice. But it doesn't work with your life. So let it go to a place where it will be loved and used and appreciated. Think of it this way: What if I told you that I had a wonderful friend who was in need of that exact nice thing? You'd probably hand it right over.

I have been amazed by how often this tactic works: a client is filled with the desire to keep something that she never uses, and I say, "Well, you know, I have a friend who's had some hard times lately, and she could really use that exact thing." And immediately the client says, "Oh! Well, in that case, go ahead and give it to her." I don't know if it's natural generosity, or if people feel better knowing that their stuff is going to a "good home," but even just imagining some wonderful, deserving person out there waiting to find your item at the thrift store and use it and love it makes it easier to let things go. So create that person in your mind. Or maybe you know someone that you would like to give it to (today!) or perhaps, again, with faith, you could just donate it to your local charity thrift store and trust that the perfect person will find it. Plus, you have lots of other nice things that you *do* love and use — let's not be dogs in the manger, here.

> The anticipation of letting go of stuff is much worse than having the stuff be gone. In fact, once it's gone, you'll find it hard to believe it was ever there to begin with.

But it was so expensive! My friend Alan has a great expression to describe expensive things that don't work out: tuition. Tuition is the money you pay to discover that something isn't right for you. It costs a bit, but it's a valuable lesson to learn that, say, having an elliptical trainer in your spare bedroom does not inspire you to work out more often. Or that owning your own scuba equipment does not actually permit you to take more scuba vacations and it would be a lot more cost-effective to rent. So take the lesson that the tuition teaches and remember: You can afford to let it go. If you can afford to not use it all this time, you can afford to let it go.

But it was such a great deal. It wasn't a great deal if you're not using it. Congratulate yourself for being such a good bargain hunter, though — it's good to know that you can find deals when you need to.

But my mother gave it to me. The love between a parent and a child (or between friends or coworkers or sponsors or schoolmates or siblings or you and whoever gave you that thing you're not using) is not what is in question here. In fact, take a moment to think about your relationship with the person who gave you this thing you don't use. It might be a rather complicated relationship. And that's okay. You can have a complicated relationship with a person and still get rid of the thing he gave you. The thing is not his love. The thing is not your love for him. It's just a thing. A thing, may I remind you, that you do not love or use.

Also, everybody gives a dud gift every once in a while. You might have plenty of wonderful things that were given to you by that very same person — in which case you can certainly afford to get rid of the dud.

Maybe the person who gave that dud to you has died or passed out of your life. The fact that you will not receive another gift from that person is not a reason to hang on to a gift that doesn't work for you. If you need to grieve, then grieve. But don't hang on to some stuff just because you miss someone. Your present life needs the space, and I can't imagine that anyone who would give you a gift would begrudge you that space.

Go ahead and see if you can picture the person in your mind, and the person is telling you with a smile, "It's okay — I just wanted you to know that I care about you, and that's why I got you that item. I know you care about me, too, so it's okay to let it go." Sounds a little silly, maybe, but it's important to have permission to be in charge of your own life, and to have permission to be in charge of the things that take up space in your life.

I myself had a hard time getting rid of some family heirlooms until I imagined my tall, classy, no-nonsense grandmother standing next to me saying, "Sweetheart — this stuff doesn't belong in your life; it belonged in mine. Let it go. Get something better." I wept a bit, and then I did just that.

But I could sell it on the Internet or at a yard sale. You know, selling stuff is a remarkably time-consuming process. And, not to sound like a broken record, but if you really wanted to sell your stuff, you probably would have done it already.

It's perfectly natural to want to realize some profit on things you have that have value — or if not realize a profit, at least not take a *total* loss. But let's analyze here for a moment — how much money would you really get? Forty dollars? A hundred dollars? A thousand dollars? And how much time and hassle would it take to sell it privately? If you consider that your time is worth, say, twenty dollars an hour, how much profit would there be? If the amount of money is significant and the time and hassle are not too much of an issue, then go ahead and post your listing (today!). Or perhaps you can think of another way; give it to a friend to sell for you (sharing the profits, of course), or use an auction house or we-sell-it-for-you place. You will get somewhat less money, but *any* money is more than the *zero* money the item is generating by just cluttering up your space.

But it reminds me of that special time. Your memories are so precious and unique — they are just for you and exist just in your mind. They are a wonderful part of you. No one can take your memories away from you. Even if you get rid of the souvenir, you will still have the memory. Just as you can love a person and not the thing that person gave you, you can love your memories of a time or an event and not love the memento itself. If you can't quite bring yourself to get rid of it entirely, is it possible to just save part of it? Maybe just the ribbon from the bouquet? Or just the scorecard from the ball game and not the whole program? Or maybe you can take a photo of the item and put it with your special pictures so it will be there when you're reminiscing.

> Honor your past, but do not allow it to inhibit your present.

But it's a family treasure — I want to keep it for my children and my children's children. If you are lucky enough to have valuable family items that deserve preservation, then make sure you are honoring that responsibility by keeping those items clean and safe from dust, bugs, and the elements. Treat those items with respect, and invest in the proper storage for them. Acid-free tissue paper is not cheap, but if you truly want to preserve your grandmother's quilt it is a necessity. Research how to properly "bank" your items and find a safe, unobtrusive place to keep them.

If you find yourself unwilling to do the above, and you also find yourself not loving or using these family treasures, I invite you to consider the possibility that maybe the biggest gift you could give your children's children is a life unencumbered by excess.

ACTION STEP

Go to a cluttered area of your home or office and spend just five minutes sorting and tossing.

CHAPTER ELEVEN

Looking under the Rock

We've spent some time in the past few chapters looking at the practical side of breaking free of procrastination and some strategies for creating the money, time, and space to work. Now let's look at some of the deeper, less visible roadblocks you might be facing. This is the tough stuff that often doesn't get discussed in polite company: stubbornness, entitlement, jealousy, disappointment, and getting lost in comparison. Let's start with stubbornness and jump right in with an exercise.

 EXERCISE: WHAT'S KEPT YOU FROM SUCCEEDING?

Sometimes it is simply your own stubbornness and stuck thinking that are holding you back. This exercise asks you to be completely frank with yourself — asking some tough questions in a kindly voice to help you break through some of those nasty internal barriers to success. So grab a pen and, working swiftly, answer the following ten questions for yourself with as much blazing honesty as you can muster:

1. What has stopped you from succeeding before this?
2. What's your most likely form of self-sabotage?
3. If you found yourself engaging in that self-sabotage, how might you handle that?

4. What are you afraid might happen if you fail at this project?
5. How might you address the situation if that failure actually occurred?
6. What are you afraid might happen if you succeed at this project?
7. How might you address the situation if that success problem actually occurred?
8. What qualities do you possess that can help you out as you move through this project?
9. What question has not been asked that you need to answer?
10. What is the truth? (Start by writing, "The truth is...")

You may notice that imagining the worst of both failure and success, and then imagining how you might handle those eventualities, helps you feel a bit more in the driver's seat.

Fear paralyzes; curiosity cures.

Writing down the answers to these questions encourages you to give voice to the monsters that live under the bed, disarming them once and for all.

It's Not All about Talent

Here's another hard truth: your talent doesn't entitle you to anything.

You will not be surprised to learn that talent is not enough. Every artist is (or believes herself to be) talented. Talent is the price of admission, kids.

You'd be amazed how many agent/manager/gallery owner submission letters say, "I'm very talented and I think we should work together." You're talented? Whoopee. I mean, seriously, you'd better be. You're going to look pretty silly calling yourself an artist if you're not talented. So it's time to move on. You're going to need to offer more than just that.

Another problem with getting too hung up on talent is that artists sometimes feel indignant because they feel — hell, they *know* — that they are far and away the best, most talented person for a particular job, and yet they don't get selected. That can be a bitter pill to swallow. It's hard knowing you're the best choice and still be passed over.

> Your talent is God's gift to you. What you do with it is your gift back to God.
> — Leo Buscaglia

But I have noticed something: people don't always make the best choices. In the same way that you don't always choose the best food for your body, or the best shoes for your feet, or the best television show to watch, other people don't always choose the best artist for the job.

The world might be a better place if we all read only the highest-quality books, only screened the highest-quality movies, and only drove the best, most efficient cars. But "best" is not our only criterion. Sometimes convenience counts. Sometimes what's in fashion is important. Sometimes it's all about what's sexy. Sometimes a person wants a little schlock — a little artistic junk food. Sometimes cheesy is perfect.

What's best is not only relative; it's often irrelevant. So cut the people a little slack — *you* wouldn't always choose you, either.

Forget Best — What about "Adequate"?

Sometimes talent isn't even the issue. We all know artists whom we perceive to be completely without talent, and yet they make buckets of money. It's not fair, I know.

But we can't do anything about the success of other people. And we can't adjust the marketplace to suit ourselves. So my advice is to just get over it. Seriously. There are so many things in the world that we cannot control. So since you have no control, relax. Take a deep breath and shrug. Practice saying, "Oh, well."

And trust me: it is inevitable that someone less deserving will surpass you. Oh, well. It is inevitable that the media and the marketplace will appear to be totally uninterested in your particular style or genre. Oh, well.

It is also inevitable that someday things will turn your way and that you will benefit from the seemingly random exigencies of the marketplace. And on that day, you do not have to say, "Oh, well." You can say, "Yippee!" But remember — it wasn't your talent (or just your talent) that got you there.

> Rabbi Brian Zachary Mayer once delivered one of the best pieces of advice I have ever heard: *The proper response to the inevitable is relaxation.* This applies to roller coasters, childbirth, birthdays, and the fact that there is no justice in the world of art.

There Is No Shortage of Success in the World

Being jealous of or enraged at the success of others is bad karma. Plus, it's a big waste of time. There is no shortage of success in the world. They didn't get *your* success. They got *their* success. So bless them and dismiss them and bring your attention back to you. Let's talk about how *you're* going to be successful.

Let me say it again: There is no shortage of success in the world.

At no time does the world say, "Okay, that's it — no more famous people for a while." There is an endless supply of money, too. It may not be in your wallet, but it's out there. Get rid of the idea that success is scarce, and instead open yourself to the idea that success is plentiful.

And there's success out there for you. It may not look like what you think it ought to look like (in fact, I can almost guarantee that it doesn't), but it's out there and headed your way. And this success is so perfect, so

> How do you feel when you read that "success is plentiful"? Skeptical? Bitter? Enthusiastic? Relieved? How about when you think "success is on its way to me"? Notice how your body feels and how your mind reacts. You may want to spend fifteen minutes creating some art that helps get you unstuck in your thinking about success.

tailor-made for you, that you may well end up wondering how on earth you ever could have been jealous of anyone else.

The Green-Eyed Monster

It isn't the prettiest aspect of your personality, but there it is: jealousy.

Ick. How very seventh-grade of you. But all of us, no matter how far beyond seventh grade we've gotten, feel jealous sometimes.

And here's a news flash: jealousy is a gift.

Jealousy is your gut's way of telling you that first of all, whatever it is, you want some. And moreover, *you believe that you could have it.* After all, you are never jealous of those who have things you don't want.

Imagine that your best friend just added an amazing rare frog to her rare frog collection. Feel jealous? I didn't think so. If you have no interest in frog husbandry, you don't feel jealous. Mystified, maybe, about why she might want to collect frogs to begin with (in much the same way your family might feel about you and your choice of a career in the arts), but in no way jealous.

Now, if that same friend suddenly lucked into an all-expenses-paid six-month artist's retreat in a villa in Provence, you might feel jealous. Because that, you want. This is part one of the gift: the simple acknowledgment of desire.

I don't know about you, but I sometimes pretend that I don't want what I want. I pretend that things are okay with me when they aren't. I pretend to be patient when I feel impatient. I pretend I don't mind being passed over when, in fact, I mind very much.

Have you done that? Tried to quiet that "I want" voice? Hurts a bit, no?

The second half of the equation, and perhaps the more important half, is this: you believe you are capable of getting it. You are only ever jealous of things you believe you could do or have yourself.

What if your frog-loving best friend just swam the English Channel? Still not jealous, are you? Of course not, because not only do you not want to do that, but you also don't think you have the ability. But if that friend wins an award in something you think you could do, or reaches some milestone you aspire to, or obtains some neat thing that you're pretty sure you could obtain if only the circumstances were right, then that green-eyed monster light is likely to start flashing.

 ## EXERCISE: HARNESSING THE POWER OF JEALOUSY

Jealousy is a signal from within about desire and will. Add a little anger (also known by its polite name, frustration) and the recipe is complete. Again, it's not pretty, but it is an important message from your inner self — ignore it at your peril.

So the next time you find yourself trying to muzzle that nasty little voice of jealousy, take a moment and ask yourself:

1. Do I want that?
2. Why do I want that? What will getting that thing mean to me?
3. Do I think I could have it?
4. What do I think is standing in the way of my obtaining that?
5. What fifteen-minute baby steps could I take today toward that?

See if making a little progress toward your own goals doesn't turn that jealous-monster voice into a happy-cheering-look-at-me-go voice. Keep making those baby steps toward your goal, and I bet that someday soon someone might just be jealous of you.

Bouncing Back from Disappointment

Disappointment is, literally, failing to keep an appointment. Which is why I think it hurts a little more than the other bumps and bruises of life.

When you feel disappointed, you are feeling deprived of something you thought was already in motion. If you're feeling like you have an "appointment" with a promotion or a successful presentation or a new love, having that thing not work out is especially crushing because it was kind of a done deal inside your mind.

And that old saw about "don't get your hopes up, and that way you won't get disappointed" is the biggest bunch of hooey I've ever heard. First of all, it's a bad strategy because it plain doesn't work. If something you want doesn't work out, you're going to be bummed whether or not you had anticipated the failure. And missing an opportunity to have delightfully high hopes seems...churlish.

> I understand the impulse to say, "I just don't want to get hurt again." But guess what? We're here to get hurt. We're here to try again. And again. And again. We're here to gain resiliency.

So I say go ahead — get your hopes up. Dream big, lush, vivid dreams. Imagine your ideal of success with the full knowledge that reality may never measure up. Then when things *do* work out, you haven't wasted one moment tamping down your enthusiasm. And if they don't work out, well, then, you are free to feel the full force of your disappointment. Which may or may not be as bad as you had imagined it might be.

I bet that if you stacked up all your disappointments you would find that very few of them make you think, "Oh, I wish I hadn't even tried that." I bet you would mostly think, "Well, I sure learned a lot."

And that's the other thing we're here for: our soul's education.

Nevertheless, disappointments can leave deep scars. And some

There's a distinction
to be made between
disappointment and grief.
I'm not entirely sure that
you can really "get over"
grief, and I'm not sure you're
supposed to. My experience
is that most kinds of pain can
be transformed in one way
or another but that grief is
timeless and ever fresh. Over
time, waves of grief may hit
you less frequently, but when
they hit they sweep up on you
as if the loss just happened
this morning. Grief teaches us
about fragility.

disappointments take longer to heal than we'd like, even when we know we "should be over it by now." (Over it by now? Says who? What is this mysterious global time frame on getting over things? Honestly.)

Disappointment is a wise and valuable teacher. It acquaints you with grief. Grief, said the Greeks, is the daughter of anger and sadness. These two powerful emotions need to be felt, explored, and lived through. Otherwise we are only a living shadow of our true selves: pretending we don't care about the things we care about most.

So there's a time to cry and a time to stop crying.

 ### EXERCISE: THREE SIMPLE STEPS TO *REALLY* GET OVER IT

"Don't be disappointed." What a silly thing to say to a person.

After all, you can't unthink something, and you can't unfeel the way you feel about something. But you can unscrew the bolts a little bit — the ones that are keeping the idea fixed and painful.

For the free downloadable
audio "Bouncing Back
from Disappointment: Three
Strategies to REALLY Get Over
It" plus other complimentary
resources, go to
www.GetItDoneBonus.com.

Think of a disappointment you'd like to get over. Pick anything — big or small. Maybe it's just a little disappointment: You oversalted the turkey meatloaf the other night and you're a little aggravated with yourself. Or a medium one: you're still so bummed you never finished college, or that you got outbid on that house. Or a big one: you got fired. Or a really big one: you still can't believe he or she had that affair.

I just want to get a reading here: on a scale of 1 to 5, how disappointed are you about your thing?

1 = Actually, I'm mostly over it.
2 = I feel a little twinge still.
3 = It still hurts.
4 = I want to cry every time I think about it.
5 = I can't imagine *ever* being over this.

Good. The first step, as they say, is admitting that you have a problem. Being frank with yourself instead of being all good and brave is a big leap in the right direction.

Step 1. Catastrophize and Minimize

First give this disappointing event a new, more disastrous name. "I blew the presentation" can be named "Mama, I'm Headed for the Poorhouse." "I fell off my diet" becomes "I Am the Walrus" or "Baby Got Back" or "My Face Found the Ice Cream Again." Got it? Be melodramatic, and make yourself laugh.

Now write down a name that really minimizes the disappointment of the event. Spin it as if you work in politics, baby. "Nobody's buying my product" becomes "This Has Been Some Fascinating Market Research!" "I'll never get another date" becomes "Oh, Pish-posh, Silly Old Dating! Who Cares?"

Imagine you're an eccentric old person who eats blueberry pie for breakfast and doesn't give two figs about anything anybody says or does. Wave your gnarled hand and put the whole thing in perspective. We're experimenting with perspectives here, so see if you can find the truth in both the catastrophic version of events and the belittling version. If you're enjoying this, give it five more names.

155

Step 2. Look at the Bigger Picture

List three amazing blessings in your life: "My friends, the moon and stars, my husband's sense of humor."

List three major accomplishments in your life: "I run my own business, I read a lot, I'm a loyal and attentive friend."

Flexibility in narrative is a wonderful life skill.

List one reason that your disappointment wasn't all bad; find one upside: "At least I don't have to sit in that horrible office anymore." "Well, I should probably cut down on the turkey meatloaf anyway."

Step 3. Give It Over

Close your eyes and let your imagination take you to a very safe, clear mental space. Breathe. Just relax for a moment and enjoy the view, if there is one. Notice how calm and lovely it is here.

There is a presence here, too — a wise, forgiving, loving presence. Maybe it has a body or a shape, maybe not. Feel the love and comfort emanating from this presence. In a warm voice, the presence says, "I'm so sorry you've been sad. But you're going to have to give it all to me now." And suddenly there is a huge scrapbook in front of you, and as with Harry Potter's Pensieve, all the thoughts you've ever had around this disappointment magically start to file themselves away in there.

All the baby names
The color you were going to paint it
The way you were going to look
The things other people were going to say
Every last bit.
All the tears
All the anger

All the emptiness
It all goes in the scrapbook.
The horrible bits, the precious bits, the spiky, uncomfortable bits
All float effortlessly into the scrapbook.
And I do mean all of it —
Once it's in the scrapbook, there is to be
No more feeling jealous when you see
    someone else who has what you
    wanted
No more feeling sorry for yourself when
    you remember you don't have it
No more secret martyrdom.
Every last bit goes into the scrapbook
And you hand it over to the presence
And you know it is safe and gone from
    you forever.
Breathe a few deep breaths to come back
    to here and now.
How do you feel?

> Participating in the present moment while believing things should be different is like having sex while holding a grudge. You can't enjoy either one. So you've got to set down the grudge, the disappointment, and the regret that you've held in your grasp and grab the present moment with both hands. Your life deserves both hands.

You may want to spend fifteen minutes creating some art that reflects your new, lighter relationship with your former disappointment.

Our Dreary Little Seeds Do Not Compare Well to Other People's Gardens

We look at other people's work, at their creations, and we sigh in admiration.

How can it be so easy for them? Where did they find the time? Where did they find the inspiration? Where did they get their artistic sensibility? How can they have accomplished such great work? And how on earth did they manage to make such a splash and have everyone *notice* their great work?

It's enough to make you throw your head into your hands.

But here's the secret: we look at other people's work and all we see is the flower in full bloom. We look inside ourselves and all we see are the seeds.

You must trust that your seeds, with proper tending, will grow and flourish and serve to impress and inspire. And I can guarantee that your seeds are entirely different from anyone else's. Your garden will look completely different. And your "growing season," if you'll permit me to extend the metaphor, will be entirely different. You don't know how another artist works and slaves and worries and gives up and starts again — all you see are the results. And no one knows how you work and slave and worry and give up and start again. Because your work and your process are yours and yours alone.

This is another good reason to keep track of your progress (see the Weekly Project Tracking exercise in chapter 3): so you don't get distracted by the greener grass on the other side of the fence or by the beautiful flowers that unintentionally intimidate your little seedlings.

Sometimes We Get Stuck in Regret

I should have done things differently.
Now it's too late.
I've missed my chance.
I screwed it up.
I should have known.

I say: baloney. You did the very best you could do under the circumstances and with the information you had at the time. Honestly, I'm not sweet-talking you with some feel-good mumbo jumbo here

— I'm serious. As I've said, in my experience everyone is always doing the best they can do — and if they could do better, they would.

So we need to bless the past. We need to settle in to the reality that the past cannot be any different from what it is.

We need to look back and realize that we have, indeed, always done the best we knew how to do — even when our best wasn't very good. And that if the universe is friendly, we can assume it's all been, somehow, correct. We can wish things were different, but we might as well wish the mountains would walk down to the sea, because in this very moment, they can't be any different.

The past cannot be any different from what it is.

Sometimes something happens that hurts us so deeply we think it can't be right — it *must* be bad. We do something awful to someone we love. We ignore our intuition and we stay in some bad job, relationship, or situation longer than we should. We are caught in some life circumstance that feels just horrible.

I'm not saying we should paint those situations pink and call them cheerful. That would be diminishing, disrespectful, and cold. You are allowed to feel as hurt as you are, as angry as you are, as sad as you are, as disappointed as you are.

Do whatever you need to do to express those feelings in a safe way (bash the mattress with a Whiffle bat, pray, cry, run, write, sing, apologize), and if you need help to move through those feelings, for heaven's sake, set aside your pride/skepticism/reluctance and get some.

And once we've worked through all our emotions, we are still left with the truth: the past is what it is, and it cannot be different. Often, having discharged our pent-up emotion about the past, we can even see how it really was for the best — how whatever happened was a valuable (if painful) lesson for us, and we can genuinely feel grateful for the experience.

Even in the case of loved ones dying, well, we have to know that as much as it saddens us to lose time with our beloveds, we all have to die. Even with everything we know about medicine and prevention and safety, illness, death, and accidents still happen — in just the same way that unlikely healings and miracles and near misses still happen.

So we are humbled by our lack of control, and we bow our heads and still our hearts and say, "It is what it is." And it cannot be any different, no matter how hard we wish it were so. We can cling to the fantasy that it's possible to change the past, or we can declare the past the past, deal with our current feelings (whatever they may be), and move on. The past is what it is, and we can move on from here.

ACTION STEP

Repeat after me: I can move on from here.

A Prayer for Hoping against Hope

And as you stand there
Hands clasped in front of you
Eyes downcast
Concealing the disobedient pounding of your heart
It dawns on you:
Here we go again.
And while you no longer allow yourself the long, elaborate
daydreams in which everything works out perfectly,
You catch yourself thinking: Well, it could happen.
And though you have long since given up making bargains
with God,
You find yourself whispering: Please.
And since you have — years ago — quit telling
Anyone anything about anything
Because honestly,
The things people say, such as,
"Oh, it will happen for you, I just know it!"
Really?
"I have a friend who went through the same thing and then one
day, just like magic…"
Really?
"The minute you stop wanting it, that's when it will happen."
Oh. Okay.
So you haven't told a soul.

Except, after long consideration, your very dearest best friend.

And you know the odds are against you.

And still

You know that life is not a numbers game and

The Lord does, indeed, move in some very mysterious ways and

Haven't you earned —

And there you stop short.

Because life is also not about earning or deserving,

Life is about mercy and grace.

And it doesn't matter how hard you've tried or how much you've sacrificed or how positive your positive mental attitude has been.

What matters is reality.

And reality says: It's possible.

So you dwell in possibility.

Between the dark and the daylight.

No longer storming off, slamming doors, and swearing, "Never again."

No longer crying out in agony because you had been so sure this was It.

No longer elated by another promising sign.

You are here.

You are here now.

Committed to enjoying the ride.

Trusting in the friendliness of the universe.

Awakened to your heart's desire.

Knowing that there is no such thing as false hope.

All hope is real.

Real. Hope. Now.

It's all we have.

And who knows?

Perhaps the best really is

Yet to come.

CHAPTER TWELVE

Why Is It So Awful When Everyone Thinks You're So Wonderful?

The chapter introduces a quick, easy, and remarkably profound technique for handling both criticism and compliments. Because, let's face it, sometimes one can be just as bad as the other.

I love your work.

Wow, your life is so perfect.

You changed my life.

Sounds great, right? All that praise and approval? Isn't that just what you've always wanted? So why do you have a horrible, sinking feeling in your stomach?

Quite a few unexpected thoughts and feelings can arise when you begin to be a successful public person:

I'm a fraud.

Everyone thinks my life is perfect and it is so not perfect — I feel awful.

Why is being so popular so exhausting?

Don't worry — you're not crazy. You're just dealing with a very wonderful problem. So let's take a look at these unexpected thoughts one at a time.

You're Not a Fraud, You're Just Bored with Yourself

Remember, your ideas are always going to seem old hat to you, because they are *your* ideas. You've thought of them already. You've been working on them for some time now. And our brains are always more interested in the Next Thing than they are in the Old Thing.

Don't let your fatigue interfere with your excitement about your work.

Of course your work is going to feel a little obvious to you. This doesn't make you a fraud. It makes you an innovator. While your ideas may seem old to you, they are brand-new to the rest of us.

When It Looks Great from the Outside but Feels Icky on the Inside

It's a very lonely feeling when everyone keeps congratulating you on how terrific your business is going while you know that you are totally broke.

Or that you and your partner have been fighting — ugly fighting.

Or that you're thinking about giving it all up and moving far away.

Or that you are struggling with depression, health issues, family crises, or some other private hell.

But you were well raised, so you slap a smile on your face and act like everything's fine, even though it's killing you. Guess what? That's the exact right thing to do. (Almost.)

Here's the thing: when you become an artist, you also become something of a public person. And for the most part, you get to manage the message that the public receives about you. You want that message to be strong, to be consistent with your "branding" (simple definition: branding is what other people think of when they think about you), and most of all, you want that message to be about them: your clients, your audience, your fans. Your public persona needs to appear smooth, calm, and professional, and you need to keep your personal heartbreaks to yourself.

While you're still in the whirlwind of change, confusion, and pain, don't tell anyone except, of course, for your intimates — the friends, lovers, and family who truly care about you and whose love for you is in no way dependent on how successful you are or aren't.

When you are feeling the knife twist of "looks-great-outside-feels-awful-inside," it is vital that you get as much private help, support, therapy, counseling, best-friend time, exercise, meditation, spiritual guidance, and practical advice as possible. Assemble your team of trusted advisers and, in confidence, talk the situation out with them.

You may want to share your story with your public after the fact — once you can tell it without crying — because it may become an important milestone for you, an important teaching moment for others, and a heartwarming part of your artistic story. Or maybe not.

> The pain you are in is a strong signal that something needs to change, so pay attention, do your research, and be brave. Remember, honey, you won't always feel this way.

The Burden of Celebrity

Susan was so excited to be the first speaker at the conference. She was pleased by the prestige and the exposure, and she knew her presentation would knock 'em sideways.

And it did.

"For three straight days, people kept coming up to me at break, at lunch, even during other people's talks, wanting to tell me how great my presentation was and how much it meant to them. It was exhausting and sort of embarrassing. I ended up scurrying to hide in my hotel room every chance I got, because I didn't know how to handle the pressure," she said.

Here's the thing: when people are telling you about how wonderful you are, it isn't really about you. It's about them. It's about the experience they want to have of you.

Even if they are there to deliver a compliment, the compliment isn't really for you. After all, they are not giving you a compliment because they think you need one — they are giving you a compliment because they need to give one. Think about it: if you had to make conversation with Steven Spielberg at a party, would you tell him how great his movies are because you think he needs to hear the compliment? Of course not. You would tell him because *you* want the experience of giving Mr. Spielberg a compliment. True?

Compliments are, at bottom, great news. You want people to want you, to be interested in what you have to say, and to care when you're in the room. As a public person, you need to be prepared for an avalanche of attention that is based on everybody wanting something from you. Frankly, it can be something of a marathon.

So, when you have a public event coming up, train for it.

Get a lot of rest. Drink lots of water. Eat food that is healthy and sustaining. Limit your time "on the floor," and if you can, hire a stage manager-ish person who can tell people that you need to take a break now but that you'll be available later on, or that they can submit questions online, or whatever.

> Other people's attention is a high-quality problem to have. Be generous. Be attentive. Be grateful.

Susan realized that being the star of the conference was a blessing and after that first experience she got better at marshaling her energy and staying present to greet her attentive fans. "After all," she said, "I'd rather be tired from everyone wanting to talk to me than be wide-awake and have no one care!"

Most of all, you want to make sure that the person they are praising is the real you, not some manufactured version of you. But what if you're shy? How much should you let people in on the real story?

Being Authentic without Showing Your Undies

We hear things like:

Be real.

Be authentic.

Be personal.

And

It's not about you.

Nobody cares what you had for lunch.

Keep your opinions to yourself.

So how exactly do we follow all these rules? How do we be both personal and real without oversharing?

First, let's make a distinction between the private and the personal. *Private* refers to the details of your private life, which are, let me assure you, interesting only to you and to the other people who are engaged with you privately (e.g., your family and friends).

Personal refers to the kind of person you are — your personality. This, I can assure you with equal confidence, is fascinating to almost everyone.

Because we love other people. We love learning about other people's characteristics and we love comparing ourselves to them. As much as we may sometimes wish that everyone would just go away, we still want to watch more movies and read more stories and hear more music and peek in through the blinds and find out more more more about all the other people on the planet. We're hooked. And if you start telling the truth about who you are as a person, we'll be hooked on you.

Let me give you an example. Say we had a meeting scheduled and I came in late. (Not cool.) And then by way of apology, I said, "I'm so sorry I'm late. You see, my cat had to go to the vet and my

Honda has a funky seat belt and my shoelace came untied and my alarm..."

Now I am both late and tiresome. (Totally not cool.)

If, however, I were to arrive late and say, "I'm so sorry I'm late. I was, as my grandmother would say, 'trying to put five pounds of sugar into a four-pound bag.' My apologies."

It's still not cool that I'm late, of course, but I have taken the opportunity of my mistake to let you in on some things about my personality.

I've let you know that I'm the kind of person who often tries to do too much, and also that I'm self-aware enough to admit it without excuses. I've implied that I was close to my grandmother, who was both wise and pithy. I've demonstrated that I am emotionally mature enough to know when an apology is warranted but not suffering from such extreme low self-esteem as to grovel over a single infraction.

See the difference?

In the first example, I'm telling you facts and details that don't have anything to do with you or with our relationship. In the second example, I'm communicating my values, my personality, and my sense of humor, and I'm keeping my focus on how my personality might affect you and our relationship.

Let's look at another example. You know when you're on the phone listening to horrible your-call-is-important-to-us noise as you get transferred from one inattentive person to another and you become increasingly enraged with each passing moment?

I have found that the only way to deal with the dehumanizing effect of all that non-service-oriented "customer service" is to find ways to remind the person on the other end that we are both real, live people. So I might say something like, "I know I seem really wrought up about this, but I was one of those artsy-caring-and-sharing-free-to-be-you-and-me kids, and all the 'that's just our policy, ma'am' stuff makes me crazy. And I'm sure it can't be fun for you to feel like you're just a machine spouting a script either, so could we just talk like real people for a minute?"

Again, saying something like this acknowledges the truth of who you are as a person (and notice that you've always been this way — too sensitive, too revolutionary, too intense, too shy, too whatever-you-got-criticized-for-as-a-child), and you've recognized the humanity of the other person.

This technique doesn't always work, of course, but it's worth a try. Another good strategy is to ask the Unhelpful Person, "What would you do if you were me in this situation?" That usually gets at least a laugh, and sometimes it yields a great solution.

What does this mean for you talking about yourself and your work? It means that you share vivid metaphors rather than boring data. Your company's Facebook post or blog could start out something like, "My day has been like a long, hot day at a grimy carnival and I didn't even win the purple teddy bear" rather than, "I'm stressed out because X project is due and my back hurts from the skateboarding accident yesterday."

Remember — your friends and family care about the details. But your public cares about you. Or they will, once you start sharing the truth about you, the person, and keeping to yourself the details of your private life.

Let me know how it goes, okay? (I'm curious like that.)

(See what I did there?)

Okay. Now go be you.

Taking It Personally

Managing your private and public personas can be a bit of a tightrope walk, but just as if you were an aerialist, keeping your head up, your eyes forward, and a slight Mona Lisa smile on your face will help keep you in balance, no matter what else is happening in the circus around you.

As ferocious as your self-criticism can be, the words of another can scar you for life. Even the softest and best-intentioned comments can set off a bomb. You've probably taken some heat about this over the years. "Don't be so sensitive." Or "Don't take everything so personally." Which is ridiculous. Of course you're going to take it personally.

Here's a quick insight: everybody else is taking everything personally, too.

Which, when you think about it, is sort of funny, because I would guess that 97 percent of what other people say to you has absolutely nothing to do with you. They are speaking entirely to themselves, saying things they need to hear about situations that concern them. Nevertheless, we must deal with the remarks of others, well-intentioned or not.

The technique I am about to share is one of the most effective ways to conquer fear, self-doubt, criticism, and praise-phobia that I've ever seen. I call it the "Sometimes Game."

 ## EXERCISE: THE SOMETIMES GAME

The object of this game is to develop the ability to hang out, gracefully, with the thoughts and ideas that frighten us. This takes practice because our first impulse is to run away from such thoughts, or to repress them, or to dwell on them until they become big, horrible monsters lurking behind every shadow.

Let's get the monsters out from under the bed and then lie down next to them on the mattress. No need to cuddle. Just be there. Peacefully.

We do this so that our fears do not get put in charge of making our decisions.

A common phrase in the self-help world is "What you can't be with runs you," also sometimes expressed as "What you resist, persists." For example, if you are afraid of being rude — if you can't even handle the idea that you might be rude sometime — then the fear of rudeness will be making all your decisions for you.

Put in slightly more concrete terms, if you are terrified of spiders, then you will spend your whole life avoiding places that you think might contain spiders. But if you are able to just be with spiders (even if you don't like them), then you can go anywhere.

Note: This exercise can call up some deep feelings, so I urge you to be take good psychic care of yourself as you do the work, and afterward. I know you'll only go as deep as is emotionally safe for you to go, so don't worry that this is risky in any way, but you might want to keep a box of tissues and a big glass of water nearby.

Step 1. Write Out the Hurtful Thoughts

To play the Sometimes Game you need to write down something, right off the top of your head, that someone might say about your work that would really, truly hurt your feelings. Maybe it's something like "You are such a fraud" or "Your work is boring."

Next, you must write down something that your Imaginary Parent might say to you that would really hurt your feelings. This might be something that an actual parent might say or has said, but I'm more interested in the voice of the Imaginary Parent inside your mind. Feel free to write a statement down for each if you'd like.

Perhaps you've written down "You are such a disappointment to me" or "You're revolting."

Finally, write down something that an Imaginary Lover might say to you that would be kind of mean. Again, it may be something that you've heard in real life, but not necessarily.

Maybe something like "You're ugly" or "You're a lousy kisser."

Step 2. Add the Word *Sometimes*

Now go back, rewrite each sentence in the first person ("I am..." instead of "you are...," etc.) and add the magic word *sometimes* to the end of each one:

So now you can read your first sentence as, "I am such a fraud... sometimes."

Say that sentence out loud.

Let it circulate through your system. Breathe it in, then exhale it.

Is there any way in which this is true? Even a little?

Can you remember a time when you were a fraud?

When someone you love was a fraud?

For me, the answer is always "Yes."

It's always at least a little bit true sometimes. I can always remember a time when, intentionally or not, I was fraudulent. Not my favorite memory, but there you have it.

When I start to feel like I can peacefully coexist with this idea — that someone could say to me, "You are such a fraud sometimes" and I would respond, "Yes, that's true," then I move on to the next sentence.

Same thing: "My work is boring... sometimes."

Is it true? Oh, hell, yes.

I bore myself to tears sometimes. And I notice that sometimes other people bore me, too. I'm sure I've bored others. Yep.

Keep going until you have reduced or eliminated your resistance to each thought.

Step 3. Write Out the Loving Thoughts

Now — this is the fun part — we're going to do the same thing with compliments.

Write down the single nicest thing you can imagine anyone saying about your work — something that would make you blush furiously and paw the floor.

Maybe it's something like "Your work is inspirational" or "You are the best in the world!"

And what might your Imaginary Parent say that would just thrill you to your bones? Something truly wonderful like "You bring me nothing but joy."

And, finally, your Imaginary Lover — what might he or she say that would make you grin? "Your love transforms me" or "You are the sexiest person ever!"

Step 4. Add the Word *Sometimes* Again

Now change the sentences to first person, add the magic word *sometimes* to the end of each one, and read them aloud:

"My work is inspirational...sometimes."

"I am the best in the world...sometimes."

"I bring nothing but joy...sometimes."

"I am the sexiest person ever...sometimes."

Is it true? Sometimes? Can you see it?

Learning how to accept both the praise and criticism of others — and please notice I said "accept" because you don't have to *agree* with them, you just have to accept them — is an important part of becoming spiritually and creatively mature.

After all, if your work is going to have an impact on the world, that means some people are really going to like it.

And some people won't.

Use the Sometimes Game any time someone says something that pushes your buttons, and you will find yourself becoming a calmer and more gracious person.

By the way, I can almost guarantee that the thing of yours that turns out to be the most popular will not be your favorite piece. For sure. It'll be the piece that you look at and think, "Really? Hmm...not my best work." But that's okay — don't get caught up in that. Other people get to like what they like.

MY ONE PIECE OF HATE MAIL

This "sometimes" strategy has served me well over the years, and never more so than when I got my first, and so far only, piece of hate mail.

It was an email from someone I knew a little bit, and liked — a musician named Josh. He and I had some mutual friends and had once both performed at a house concert sort of event. We spoke afterward, and he had some very flattering things to say about my writing, and I admired his songs. We were quite friendly, but at the time I received this hate mail, I hadn't seen him in several years.

He was responding to what I thought was a fairly innocuous email touting my book of poetry, and while I no longer remember his exact words, he wrote me back an email that included these phrases: "You are such a fraud. Does anyone buy your authenticity? I can't wait to pull back the curtain on you. You prey on people's dreams."

Ouch.

Step 1. Walk away from the computer and wait twenty-four hours before responding.

Whenever someone pushes your buttons, make sure you wait for the inevitable ego flare-up to subside. Don't try to *not* have the ego flare-up — as I said, it's inevitable. Just let all those feelings of hurt and injustice and rage wash over you and then roll out like the tide.

Step 2. Ask yourself, Is it true?

As I reread Josh's remarks, I noticed something: the accusations that I felt to be completely untrue didn't hurt my feelings one bit.

"Does anyone buy your authenticity?" Um, yes. Pretty

much everyone. It's one of the comments I hear most often — what a "real person" I am. So that one felt to me as though he had said something almost nonsensical, like, "You're from Florida!" Um, no, I'm not. But whatever, dude.

And as for "pulling back the curtain" on me, I felt more mystified than hurt. "Sure," I wrote back, "come on over! I'll show you my checkbook and my datebook and my email database and anything else you want to see. Honestly, there's not really much of a curtain to pull back."

"You prey on people's dreams." That one was tougher. I could sort of play with the words so it would mean "I *pray* on people's dreams," which is much nicer, but I was committed to finding the truth, if any, in what he said. I did the Sometimes exercise and sat with it for a good long while.

Finally I wrote back to him: "Yes. In a way, you are right. I do have a business in which I help people identify and move forward on their dreams. And that business does buy my groceries. So, while I wouldn't choose to put it that way, I do prey on people's dreams."

And I thanked him for giving me the opportunity to go deep — to sit with the very darkest interpretation of what I do. It was a valuable investigation for me, and I found a new assurance in my work by spending time on the idea that while my work could be thought of as craven and predatory, I knew my motives were pure.

Josh wrote me back the next day, appalled — he had sent his email to the wrong person! He thought he was writing to someone else named Sam, a devious music producer who'd been duping young, unsigned musicians into paying "management fees" with vague promises of record deals and "connections" and thus cheating them out of thousands of dollars.

Now, I don't know what email angels were at work to divert Josh's email to me, and I honestly don't think anyone should go around writing emails like that no matter what the provocation, but the lesson remains: it's not about you.

And the part that *is* about you is yours to investigate, honor, and find the truth in. Sometimes.

It's Okay to Make Nice with Yourself

> It's time to give those chattering critical voices in your head a rest. It's time to change the tape. It's time to accentuate the positive. If it doesn't work, no worries — you can always go back to thinking negatively any time you'd like.

Guess what? It's okay to have some positive thoughts about yourself. Many of us were raised in intellectual households, where if you couldn't prove your point, well, you were just being delusional. I'm asking you to be a little delusional. You may be reluctant to think nice thoughts about yourself. I understand. You may feel that your negative thoughts "keep you in line" and you don't want to "get a big head."

Darling, you will not get a big head. I promise.

 ### EXERCISE: TEN NICE THINGS

Step 1. Write Down Ten Successes, Wins, or Blessings from the Past Year

Grab a pen and write down ten good things that have happened in the past twelve months. They can be things that you made happen

("I paid off all my credit cards" or "I learned how to cook a perfect roast chicken"), things that happened to you ("My cousin gave me that wonderful birthday present" or "I got asked to perform the solo"), things that happened around you ("There is some jasmine growing right next to my bedroom window, and it smells heavenly" or "Those noisy neighbors finally moved away") or (most likely) some combination of the above.

Don't have a contest with yourself about the "best" things that happened to you; just list some things that, when you reread the list, make you nod and smile to yourself and think, "Yep. That's pretty good."

Step 2. Write Down Ten Nice Things about Yourself

Now make a list of ten nice things about you. They may be nice qualities that you were born with, like your quick mind and your lovely eyes. They may be nice skills you've learned, like your gorgeous gardening skills and your ability to run a mile without losing your breath. Or maybe they're things other people appreciate about you, like what a safe and courteous driver you are, and how you always remember everyone's birthday.

Push yourself to come up with ten.

After all, the assignment is not to write down ten extraordinary things about you, or ten things that no one else in the world has ever done — just ten nice things that, again, you can look at and say, "Yep. That's pretty good."

How to Have a Conversation with Well-Meaning People

Great job. This is a fun exercise to do not only because it reminds you that your life is not all drudgery and areas that need improvement but also because it gives you some talking points for the next time someone asks you, "So, how's it going?"

We need talking points, or go-to conversational gambits, because people are always putting artists on the spot. "How's the book going?" "Had any good auditions lately?" "Are you still working on that one piece?"

Sigh.

We know in our hearts that people inquire because they are interested, because they love us, because they can't possibly imagine doing what we're doing and they're curious about how a project like ours might go, and because they don't know what else to say. After all, they're pretty sure we don't want to talk stock options.

Anyway, they are not trying to put us on the spot or make us feel bad about our progress or lack thereof — even though when they ask we feel put on the spot and we feel bad about our progress or lack thereof. We think that if we don't have some fabulous recent success to share that we have somehow failed. And that's just not true.

Whatever the reason, any time you don't feel like answering a question someone asks, just use the old PR trick of answering the question you *wish* he had asked. If you're in the middle of working on a piece, and someone asks how it's going, take advantage of the lists you've just made, smile, and say, "Oh, it's great. You know, I'm pretty quick minded, so I've been learning to slow down by gardening. Let me tell you about my zucchini and my zinnias!" That's right. I'm recommending that you change the subject abruptly.

You can maintain control of a conversation without being rude, and you have the right to not answer directly if you don't want to. And now you are not only having a nice conversation, but you are also reminding yourself that you are a nice person and good things happen to you. Since you're going to be thinking something anyway, why not think those things?

Note: The "ten nice things" lists are also useful in an interview situation, on a first date, in cover letters, in personals ads, and on webpages and bios and anywhere else you are being asked to "tell a little about yourself."

How to Have a Conversation with Well-Meaning Family Members

We all have our family of origin, and then we have our family of friends. It's one of the great perks of adulthood — you get to pick a second family of friends who love you. While it's likely that both these families love you and care about you and want the best for you, you may have noticed that most of them neither know nor care much about your work.

They don't understand what you do. They don't understand why you do it. It probably even seems kind of crazy to them.

That's okay. Your family is in your life to love and support you as a person — they are not here to be your audience, your clients, or your critics.

Do not expect *anyone* to have any understanding of what you do or why. After all, do you understand why firefighters actually choose to run into burning buildings? Or why neurosurgeons elect to put their hands inside someone's brain? Of course not. We're just damn grateful they do.

Same with art. People who are not artists haven't got the faintest idea what it's like to be you. And people who aren't parents can't really know what it's like to have kids, and people who've never suffered from depression can't imagine how bleak life can seem — you see where I'm going with this?

So if your family bums you out by saying ignorant or disparaging things about your work, just keep your head down and your shields up and change the subject.

For the free 60-minute downloadable bonus audio "Why Is It So Awful When Everyone Thinks I'm So Wonderful?" plus other complimentary (and complementary) resources, go to www.GetItDoneBonus.com.

ACTION STEP

Think of someone who has made you angry or whose behavior has upset you, and write down ten nice things about him or her (you can add the word *sometimes* if it helps you). Notice how you feel, and, if your feelings are very powerful, consider making some art about the situation.

CHAPTER THIRTEEN

Do You Quit When You're Almost Done?

If you want to make a creative person feel bad, just ask her about the projects she's left undone.

But here's a revolutionary thought: sometimes completion is overrated.

That is to say, some projects are valuable only for their process, and finishing them is unnecessary. Take journaling, for example. Journaling is valuable only for the act of journaling, not for the result of having a bunch of journals.

And sometimes we're just experimenting. So you might start writing a screenplay, get fifteen pages in, and realize that this is just not your medium. Great. You have my permission to ditch it.

But maybe you find yourself quitting on things you really would love to finish. What then? Pooping out two-thirds of the way through happens to everyone. Everyone. Push past this point of resistance, and watch miracles happen. If nothing else, watch the miracle of your having pushed yourself past the point where you might otherwise have given up.

> Why do I talk about the benefits of failure? Simply because failure meant a stripping away of the inessential. I stopped pretending to myself that I was anything other than what I was, and began to direct all my energy into finishing the only work that mattered to me.
>
> — J. K. Rowling

Below we'll discuss a few ways to help you reach the finish line.

Get a Bigger Carrot

Find some affordable incentive that makes it more pleasurable to finish your project. For example, if you send in your book proposal by April 1, you get to spend three days at the beach. Even small tasks can benefit from a bigger carrot.

When faced with a troublesome phone call that must be made, I often promise myself that I can go back to bed and read for half an hour once I've made the call. (This is the beauty of working from home: so many of my rewards feature going back to bed.)

Get a Bigger Stick

Find a way to make it more painful not to finish. For example, you hand a trustworthy friend a check for $500 and tell him that if you don't show him a completed book proposal by April 1, he gets to send the money to the social or political cause with which you most disagree. I first learned this strategy ten years ago from my dear friend Amy Ahlers, the Wake-Up Call Coach and author of the bestselling *Big Fat Lies Women Tell Themselves: Ditch Your Inner Critic and Wake Up Your Inner Superstar*, and all these years later, it still tickles me.

Reduce the Scope of Your Project

"It's *big*, R.J.! Big!" says the screenwriter to the old-time Hollywood producer, and your vision may also have first appeared to you in breathtaking Cinemascope and stereophonic sound. But you may be paralyzing yourself with the grandiosity of your vision.

Reducing the size of your project might free you up. So rather than trying to create an international convention of lute lovers complete with presentations, performances, and a trade fair, perhaps you could host a gathering in your home for ten to twelve lute lovers. This strategy is especially effective for test-driving Big Ideas.

I once had a client named Virginia who had dreams of opening a dance studio. Before she knew it, she was knee-deep in commercial real estate brochures and cumbersome questions about insurance and employee compensation. She was, to put it mildly, discouraged.

After some discussion of what about her initial idea had so engaged her ("working with young artists," "bringing spirituality and dance together," and "giving real, practical help and advice — after all, I was a dancer, too — I've been there!"), she realized that she could begin by offering a one-day intensive workshop. Her church would be happy to rent her a space very inexpensively, and suddenly the idea of only having to get fifteen dancers in a room for one day seemed very doable.

Eventually, Virginia did open a dance studio that focused on the intersection of movement and spirituality, but she ended up doing it through her church, thus saving her a million administrative headaches and allowing her to focus on the part of the work that truly inspired her: teaching.

Increase the Scope of Your Project

Maybe you're stuck because you're bored. You've been thinking too small.

Perhaps rather than trying to sell your jewelry at local craft fairs, it might be more exciting to sell your items online to a global audience of moneyed fans. Maybe rather than auditioning for the local community chorus, you'd like to book an evening at a piano bar and offer your very own one-person cabaret show.

Try this: Write down a number-related aspect of your goal, then add a zero. So if you've been thinking you'd like to make $10,000, what happens when you open up to the idea of making $100,000? If you're working on selling five or ten of something, what does selling fifty or a hundred look like? Rather than trying to grow your email list a person at a time, what if you found a way to grow your list a thousand people at a time?

Thinking big gets you out of your self-imposed limitations. You stop thinking about what's possible for you to accomplish on your own, and you start thinking about what's needed for this quantum leap to happen. "What does the project need?" is a much more fruitful question than "How do I do this by myself?"

Ask any successful creative entrepreneur her secret and every single one will tell you, "I got out of the way of the vision."

ACTION STEP

Write down three to five variations in scope of your project and see which size project feels like the best fit. (Note: Don't worry about what you think you are capable of doing; just pick the one that makes your heart go thump thump thump and live with the idea for a while.)

CHAPTER FOURTEEN

Beginning to Get Your Work Out There

If you could combine the emotional punch of Daniel in the lion's den, Dorothy in front of the great and powerful Oz, and Neil Armstrong's first step on the moon, you might get a feeling in your belly that approximates the feeling of putting your work out there into the world.

Putting your work out there is terrifying. But eventually you know you're going to have to do it. Because a project that we keep to ourselves is known as a hobby.

Is It Your Hobby or Is It Your Art?

Your art is that which you feel compelled to share with the world. Your art is that which you know, in your heart, the world needs to receive in your way, in your medium. Your art is your sincere effort to help heal the world. You yourself have been healed by art. That cruddy movie that helped you get over your broken heart? That song that soothes you every time? That piece of sculpture that enraptures you? You have been healed by art, and you feel the desire to pay back the favor by sharing your work with the world.

Hobbies, on the other hand, are just for you. Hobbies are the stuff you do that entertains you, that expands your soul, that may even delight others but that is decidedly not meant to be shared with the world.

Confuse art with hobby at your own peril. To put the pressures of art on what is merely a hobby is unfair. So the next time someone sees the little quilt that you made as a baby shower gift and starts exclaiming that you should sell your quilts, feel free to smile graciously and say no. You make those quilts because you love to, and you'd hate to sully that love with any kind of imperative.

On the other hand, to deny your art its destiny and demean it by referring to it as "just my little hobby" or "this dumb little project" or "my silly idea" is cruel. So assuming you want to see your art out in the world (c'mon — it's time to quit putting on plays in the backyard!), here are some steps to help you start thinking of your work as a commodity to be marketed, whether or not you intend to charge for it.

Okay, enough theory. Let's experiment and see if we can't make a little money.

 ## EXERCISE: SEVEN EASY STEPS TO MAKING A PROFIT — TODAY!

Feel free to adjust this step-by-step process to your own taste, standards, and project. You might do this all in one day (really — you *could* do this all in one day), or you might choose to spread it out over a few days.

> Being good in business is the most fascinating kind of art. Making money is art and working is art and good business is the best art.
> — Andy Warhol

And if you elect not to try this (which is totally fine, of course), I still want you to think about what you might do if you *were* to try it. Deal? Deal.

Step 1. Pick a Product

Think of something you have already created that you think would benefit people. Maybe it's a story or a song, maybe it's a print, a product, a poster, or an audio recording.

If you're not sure, ask someone who's familiar with your work, since sometimes others will remember things we don't. You might hear things like "Oh, you should sell that talk you give on how to organize your desk — that's great stuff!" or "What about those T-shirts you designed on Zazzle.com?" (And here you had forgotten all about those T-shirts...)

> By the way, Zazzle.com and CafePress.com are two websites that allow you to design and sell a product without ever having to pay set-up costs or buy inventory. You set your own royalty, and they can "host" your "shop." It's pretty fun.

You can host virtual or digital products on your own website, of course, and there are also online resources that will allow you to build an easy-peasy site without even having your own domain name. And if you're wondering how to create a recording, there are plenty of free conference calling resources online, too, where you can just dial in, hit record, and go for it!

If you don't already have something you can repurpose, then just imagine yourself ten years ago. What information (related to your project) do you dearly wish you had had? What insights would have been helpful to you?

So, for example, Steve might say, "Three things you need to know about becoming a TV writer in Los Angeles," or Sam might say, "How to price your product...and what to do about refunds." Great. And of course I want you to give this product a name that delights you, but don't get too clever with it. When it comes to product names, it's best to be clear. Write down your product name now.

Step 2. Get Ready for Your Debut

If your product is all ready to go, then great! You can skip this step. If your product is almost ready, then complete whatever's necessary to get a beta version out the door. Spend less than an hour on this. Turn the Word doc into a pdf, add a graphic element, slap your logo on it, edit out the boring introduction — whatever. And really, set the bar low.

No, lower. Seriously…lower it some more. Okay, that's good.

Step 3. Prepare to Profit

Set your price about a third higher than you think it should be.

If you're nervous about that, offer a satisfaction-guaranteed-or-your-money-cheerfully-refunded policy. After all, you know you're going to overdeliver.

If you need to, do fifteen minutes (only!) of research on how other similar products are priced. But don't compare your work to mass-produced items. The stuff sold in the big-box stores might be cheaper, but it is not handcrafted by you. You bring a lifetime of skills and talents to your work, so just because someone can buy a greeting card for a few bucks at the drugstore does not mean that you should price your one-of-a-kind watercolor cards as low.

Step 4. Deliver

Get a proper email address. If you don't already have a business email address, set one up via your website. Most website hosting services offer nearly unlimited email addresses. If that doesn't work for you, then set up a Gmail account with a professional name like "your businessnamehere@gmail.com."

Do *not* use your personal address or any "sbcglobal," "yahoo," or, heaven forfend, "aol" address. We're going bare bones, but we don't want to look like amateurs here.

Set up a way to receive payment. As of this writing, Paypal is fine. Google Checkout is also fine. Amazon Payments can also work well. Pick whichever one feels right. Of course, by the time this book is published, there will probably be some whole new way to collect payments. Again, do not spend more than fifteen minutes making this decision. Personal credit card swipers that attach to your iPad or smart phone are available for free, and I don't know why everyone doesn't get one. I mean, even if you just use it at your next yard sale it's worth having, yes?

Figure out delivery. How is your product delivered? Do you send out an email, and if so, can you use an auto-responder? Do you have to mail it out? Is it a digital product that just lives on a webpage somewhere, and you just have to communicate the address of the page?

Fulfillment houses are miraculous at printing books, posters, decks of cards, skateboards, mouse pads, aprons — you name it. They will print, wrap, and ship, and you never even have to go to the post office. Brilliant. Ask around to find a good one.

Step 5. Get It Out of the House!

Now write a brief, simple email to your people explaining that you have just released this fabulous new recording/pdf/ebook/T-shirt /workbook/video/whatever and you can't wait for them to enjoy it.

Write out three benefits a person might get from purchasing your product. Hint: Think about how the person buying your product will feel once she's gotten it. This is no time to get shy. Enlist the help of a cheerful and supportive friend if you need to.

Your benefits might be how special someone will feel purchasing such a fabulous handcrafted item directly from the artist. Or how cool he'll feel knowing that he is one of the first people to get this product. Or maybe your benefits have to do with how yummy she'll feel or how smart she'll become or how giggly she'll get or how impressed her boss will be.

If you have trouble with this, try writing down "Ten Nice Things about My Product" and see what happens.

Finally, make sure you ask for the sale. Just sending out an announcement will not help people buy. Writing "Click here to buy now!" and providing a PayPal link will help people buy.

Step 6. Press "Send"

This is far and away the scariest thing you've done in a long time, I bet. The thought of pressing "Send" will bring on dizzy spells, upset stomachs, and the urgent need to reorganize your sock drawer.

I know how hard this is, and I'm with you every step of the way. In fact, I'll even tell you a little story to help ease your anxiety.

Several years ago I started getting inquiries about my poetry. Specifically, was there a book or a collection of them anywhere? So I thought, okay, I'll make a collection.

I gathered up my writing, did some judicious editing, created a table of contents (which turned out to have an error in it — see "Don't Be Afraid to Get a C," page 45, and "Forget Best — What about Adequate," page 149), turned it into a pdf, and called it "By the Way, You Look Really Great Today: Selected Poems by Samantha Bennett." Let me tell you, too, that this little process I just described of gathering and editing was remarkably time-consuming. It took a lot longer than I thought it would, and by the end I was sort of annoyed by the whole thing.

I also found myself face-to-face with the Who-Do-You-Think-You-Are Monster, who showed up wearing the "You're Not a *Real* Writer" mask. Shoot, I get squirmy just calling my work poetry. After all, I'm no Mary Oliver.

Luckily, I have a business called the Organized Artist Company and I teach a class called Get It Done, so I'm sort of contractually obligated to not let tedium, fear, or low self-esteem stop me from producing. I screwed my courage to the sticking place, put a five-dollar price tag on the thing, and wrote an email to my list with a link for payment.

The minute before I hit "Send" was the longest minute of my life. I felt dizzy, upset, and unwell. I felt sure I had left something out. I was positive that my book needed more visuals. Maybe another poem or two. I would have done anything *not* to send it out. I wanted to cry. I did cry. Then I took a few deep breaths, reminded myself that this was all just a big experiment, said a heartfelt prayer, and pushed the button.

I went for a long walk. When I returned, I was eager to see how many orders I had.

I had zero orders.

Okay, I thought — no biggie. Probably by tonight I'll get a few. Nope.

Forty-eight hours later, I had sold exactly two copies: one to a guy in my choir and one to a woman I barely knew.

My mom hadn't even bought one.

Now, this book has gone on to sell more than $5,000 worth of copies (which makes it rather a gigantic blockbuster hit in the poetry world), and it's available still, but the lack of response to that first offer was quite a blow to my ego.

Here's what I think happened: the only person who found it in the least bit remarkable that I would be selling a book of poetry online was me. I think everyone else, including my mom, looked at that email and thought, "Well, good. Of course she's doing that," and went on with their day.

> My friend Luke Hannington is a composer who often quotes his grade-school music teacher: "Creative people create things the way apple trees make apples." Try to think of your offerings as apples, offered freely and without expectation of approval.

You've done this, too. The last time your favorite band came out with a new album did you think, "Wow, I bet this was really challenging for them"? Of course not. You thought, "It's about time."

And the same will be true for you. No one will appreciate the hard work and courage that it takes for you to get your work out there, because everyone thinks that you know how talented you are. It won't seem remarkable to them at all. In fact, they'll probably wonder what took you so long.

Step 7. Celebrate!

Hooray!

Do whatever feels right to celebrate your amazing accomplishment.

Take a walk in the sunshine, buy yourself a treat, lie down and read a book, go see a movie, take someone you adore out for a nice meal.

Whatever you do, do *not* sit at your computer waiting to see how many people buy. That's poison. Go enjoy yourself for a few hours and then check, okay?

That's it! Congratulations, you've just launched a product.

Damn, you're good.

ACTION STEP

Get your work out there today in whatever way you can. Anything goes, from emailing a three-line poem to a friend to entering a show or competition, from publishing your website to simply putting a photo of your work on Facebook: it all counts.

CHAPTER FIFTEEN

Ending at the Beginning, or Okay, Now What?

Congratulations — your project is in motion!

And while getting started can be quite a battle, keeping up your momentum is some fierce warfare indeed. (Read *The War of Art* by Steven Pressfield, a brilliant book, for more about this topic.) Especially if you know yourself to be one of those "lots-of-initial-enthusiasm-but-not-so-good-on-the-follow-through" kinds of people. You are going to need to fight, with every weapon you have, the desire to quit, to play small, to become invisible, to retreat.

I'm hoping that this book has helped you get a handle on what's going to work for you, and you're certainly going to need a variety of inducements, bribes, strategies, and tactics to keep yourself on course.

A quick word about inspirational strategies: they are dynamic. *You* are dynamic. You are engaged in a dynamic process with your project. So don't fall into the trap of thinking that one tool is all you need. And the minute a tool or strategy starts to fall flat, try something else.

One way to keep moving forward is to make things you don't want to do be more like the things you *do* like to do. For example, if I asked you do the dishes, you would have one feeling. You might have more than one feeling. But I'll bet none of those feelings would revolve around fear or worrying about whether you could do it.

If I asked you to clean out an overstuffed garage, you would

> Any time you push yourself to a new level, you're going to feel uncomfortable. Everyone does. I've worked with everybody from Academy Award winners to those right off the turnip truck, and I'm here to tell you: the level of sophistication may be different, but the anxiety is exactly the same. So don't imagine that you're the only one who gets nervous, or that someday you're going to be so competent that you won't feel the jitters. Nervous energy is just excitement in disguise.

have another feeling or set of feelings, and you might start to wonder, "Can I do this?" You might feel apprehensive, burdened, or challenged.

Notice that the tasks themselves require the same skills of cleaning, organizing, and taking decisive action. The difference is in the feeling you have based on the scope of the task. We think we can't do something that's big and scary, well, because it's big and scary.

This exercise is designed to help you transfer your feelings of success, contentment, and overall goodness to a project that might otherwise scare you.

 EXERCISE: HALLMARKS OF JOYFUL EASE

First close your eyes and bring to mind a moment when you felt particularly successful, particularly happy, and particularly good about being you. Make it a specific memory — not just "eleventh grade" but "that afternoon in the locker room after we won the volleyball game." Recall as many of the physical and emotional specifics as you can.

Step 1. Write Down the Hallmarks of the Moment

Draw a vertical line, dividing a piece of paper in half. At the top of the first column, write the heading "Hallmarks," and below it write a list of all the details about this moment that you can remember, such as:

Felt rewarded
Cool air
Joking around
Raining
Favorite blue sweater

Here are some questions to prompt your memory:

- What was the source of light at the time? A window? A lamp? The sun?
- What was the temperature? Was there a breeze?
- How were you feeling? Thrilled? Joyful? Awake? Satisfied?
- What caused those feelings? A compliment? A big win? Knowing you'd worked hard?
- Where did those feelings live in your body? As a quiver in your belly? A tingle up your spine? A sparkle in your eyes?
- How did your body feel overall?
- Who else, if anyone, was present?
- What, if anything, were you wearing?
- If someone had asked you in that moment, "What are your feelings about the future?" how might you have answered them?
- Can you put your finger on what, exactly, made that moment so satisfactory? Was it the feeling of a job well done? Or the teamwork? Or feeling truly and deeply loved?
- What else do you notice or remember about this memory? What details stand out to you?

Let yourself revel in the memory for a moment. Feels nice, huh? Remember, that memory is always there to energize and inspire you.

Step 2. Translate the Hallmarks into Inspiration for Your Project

Title the second column "Inspiration (a way I might use this now)."

Now see if you can transfer some of the elements from the first column into the second. For example, if your project is to complete a chapter of a novel, and one of the memory notes says, "Favorite blue sweater," you could remind yourself to put on some comfy, favorite clothes before you start writing. It might sound silly, but it's possible that by increasing your level of physical comfort you can find the courage to leap over that first hurdle and start writing.

Some elements might just be reminders of ways you like to feel. For "Joking around" you might find a way to remind yourself of your lightheartedness and humor while working. Other elements may not transfer directly, so use your imagination. If your memory includes "Raining," that may just remind you to look up at the sky before sitting down to work.

This exercise is a reminder about what you value, and the circumstances under which you feel most fully and comfortably yourself — which is valuable information for you and your muse.

People have also used this exercise to remind themselves about transferring the skills they already have. If, for example, calling friends to invite them to a party feels easy and fun, then maybe rather than sending an email to get new clients, it might better suit you to call them, imagining your business offerings as a new kind of "party."

Transferring feelings of joy and ease to new and potentially scary situations will give them the hallmark feelings of success.

THE BLUE SUIT

My favorite story about this exercise comes from a tall, handsome fellow named Geoff. Geoff took my Get It Done Workshop because he had to make a phone call.

Don't laugh — we've all been there.

There's a phone call that you know you have to make but you don't make it and then more time passes and it becomes even more embarrassing that you haven't made it and so you are even more reluctant but you still have to call and the pressure builds and it starts to feel more and more horrible that you haven't called so you still don't call although you know you really must but by now you can't even imagine what you would say to address the fact that you've been so remiss in calling, so you just continue to not call, every day feeling worse and worse about it.

Sound familiar?

After getting clear on what exactly he wanted and why, using the Pure Preference worksheet and doing the Hallmarks of Joyful Ease exercise, Geoff decided to place his phone call while wearing a suit — he had been wearing a suit in his Hallmarks of Joyful Ease memory.

Geoff was an actor, and the call he had to make was to his agents. Three months earlier his wife had given birth to twins, and since they already had two young children, Geoff, already a devoted father, had become completely immersed in sweatpants-wearing daddyland. Putting on a suit to check in with his agents was his first step in reestablishing himself as a professional after his self-imposed paternity leave.

Of course, his agents were thrilled to hear from him and insisted that he come in that very day and bring pictures of the babies. So Geoff wore his suit to the meeting.

Get this: his agents had never seen him in a suit before. They oohed and aahed over the photos, and they also oohed and aahed over this "new" Geoff. Immediately they stopped thinking of him as a schlubby-adorable-dad type and started sending him out for parts in which he could play the hard-hearted attorney, the idealistic young senate candidate, and executives of all stripes. (The old saying "dress for the job you want, not for the job you have" goes double for artists.)

That phone call — and that suit — started Geoff's career in a totally new and lucrative direction.

GOOD DAY, SUNSHINE

Edith, another student, was the mother of a little girl named Delilah who'd been born with a severe genetic disorder that necessitated a series of surgeries throughout her young life and caused some developmental disabilities.

Edith's Hallmarks of Joyful Ease memory was of Delilah's final surgery, a long and tricky one with an uncertain outcome. She remembered the waiting room as chilly and airless, with no windows, just the cold fluorescent light on the ceiling. Although tired and worried and physically uncomfortable, she said that when the doctors came in to tell her that Delilah's surgery had been a success, Edith felt a powerful rush of energy run through her body. "If we can get through this," she thought, "we can get through anything."

Now the task Edith was facing — her project — was dealing with the boxes of medical files and insurance forms incurred by Delilah's treatment. It was a big, tedious, hairy job, but it had to be done. So Edith took a look at her Hallmarks memory and turned it on its head. She put a card table and chair next to her big patio doors so she could do her work in the sunlight and look out into the garden. She made sure she was wearing her favorite cozy sweater, and she put on her favorite Beatles albums (yes, albums — Edith is a bit of an audiophile and a connoisseur of vinyl) and then made sure that she got up and took a short break at the end of each album side.

It took the entire six weeks of the Get It Done course, but by carrying the thought "If we can get through this, we can get through anything," eventually Edith got all Delilah's records in order and the insurance claims processed. Delilah is now a bright, beautiful ten-year-old making swift progress in school. She'll never be quite like any of the other kids, but she is so special that no one would want her to be.

Here are a few other discoveries my clients have made while doing the Hallmarks of Joyful Ease exercise.

Rob was a violinist whose memory involved having a wallet full of money. After doing this exercise he made it a policy to make sure he had $100 cash in his wallet for every audition — even if he had to go to the bank, take out the cash, and run it right back after the audition — because knowing he had that cash on hand increased his sense of confidence, presence, and worth.

Jane's early training was in scenic design, and her memory involved sitting in a darkened theater looking at the lit stage. She decided that in order to stimulate her creative thinking while finishing up some very boring contracts she would turn off all the lights in her house except for one strong light over her desk.

Liz's memory involved a great feeling of camaraderie; in a terrific intuitive leap, she decided to have softball jerseys printed up with her business name on the back so that all her vendors and clients could become a member of her "team."

Deirdre's memory was quite sensuous and sexy; we laughingly suggested that she should wear fancy underthings when she organized her files. The next week she came in beaming: she had cleared out and prioritized all her papers — wearing lingerie!

Here's another imagination exercise that might surprise you. (I know some of you dislike these kinds of exercises — you feel like you "can't think of anything" — and that's okay. Just try it.)

 ## EXERCISE: YOUR CREATIVE TWIN

Play along with me and let's see what happens in this visualization exercise.

Take three deep belly breaths and imagine yourself walking somewhere pleasant. As you walk, you realize that you are near a large creativity center where all kinds of artists are working, playing, performing, practicing...and you are welcome to go exploring.

Notice what your creativity center looks like. Is it a warehouse? An old brownstone? A Renaissance Faire–type atmosphere? Hear the sounds of people working, and as you walk through the space, notice what's around you. What draws your attention?

Now, coming across the way and waving wildly at you, is your Creative Twin.

Your Creative Twin is like you, but also different. First of all, your Creative Twin is rich. Really rich. Super-crazy rich. And your Creative Twin is also a bit impulsive and free-spirited.

Your Creative Twin has been known to do things like buy a villa in Tuscany sight unseen and then lend it out to a friend of a friend. Your Creative Twin has gone off for six months to study traditional Japanese dance and has created art installations in the desert that can only be seen by helicopter.

Notice what your Creative Twin is wearing, and how your Creative Twin walks and moves through the world.

Your Creative Twin greets you with great enthusiasm and perhaps calls you by a special nickname. Together you walk around the creativity center, admiring the artisans and catching up. Suddenly your Creative Twin stops short — inspiration has struck! Your Twin says, "I know! We must do a project together! This is perfect!" And your Twin begins to outline the project. Notice how you feel about this idea.

The day is winding down, and it's getting time for your Creative Twin to jet off. As you say good-bye, your Twin gives you a word of advice.

Then your Twin gives you a gift that you didn't know you needed.

Notice how you feel about the advice and the gift. Place the gift somewhere for safekeeping, and wave good-bye to your Twin.

Take one last look around your creativity center, noticing any final thoughts or niggling feelings.

Take another deep belly breath and come back to the present moment.

Now complete the following sentences about what you noticed. Perhaps one small idea will bubble up, or maybe the ideas will percolate and tomorrow you might have some blazing insight. Or maybe not. Either way, just let your mind stay blank as you write down your thoughts.

My "creativity center" was:

What caught my eye was:

My Twin was:

My Twin's name was:

The project my Twin suggested was:

My reaction was:

My Twin's gift to me was:

My Twin's advice to me was:

A real-world version of this project might be:

Other things I noticed were:

_____

Some students have wept with relief at encountering this freer, wilder version of themselves. Others have felt a little put-off, or just plain jealous that their Creative Twin had so much money and was so blithe about it. There's no right or wrong way to feel.

Take the parts of this exercise that inspire you, tickle you, or maybe seriously annoy you and play with them. See what comes up.

Perhaps your Creative Twin will lead you down an unexpected path toward a glorious new future.

ACTION STEP

Notice what your Hallmarks of Joyful Ease memory and your Creative Twin have in common. Put that information to good use today.

CHAPTER SIXTEEN

The Fear of Failure
Is Perfectly Reasonable

The book that I want to write…I am wondering if it will be useful or if anyone would want to read it. What do I do with this feeling of "who cares about your work, all the effort you put in is useless"? — Sean

Every single person throughout human history — artist and otherwise — has suffered from self-doubt, secretly believes he is a fraud, and wonders if anyone will care about his work.

You are not alone.

And I've noticed that the more daring the creative idea, the more vicious and violent those critical inner voices can become. So over time, I've learned that *the louder and meaner the voices in my head are, the greater the probability that I've just had a really juicy idea.*

> **Your doubts may be part of what makes you an artist. I've heard it said that only dilettantes and amateurs never doubt their talent.**

Think of it this way: the voices in your head are trying to keep you safe. They don't want you to make yourself vulnerable. They try to scare you into inaction by telling you that no one will care about your work or that people will judge you harshly.

But art is about making yourself vulnerable.

That's kind of the point. Or at least part of the point. And let's face facts — it's possible that you will create something that other people don't care for.

Fear of failure is entirely reasonable. But it's no reason not to do your work.

As long as your work remains unwritten in your head, it has no effect on anyone. Except you. And not in a good way. Once you let your idea out of the hermetically sealed vault of your brain and out into the fresh air, it will immediately start to evolve. The minute you get it down on a piece of paper, it will change.

And once you let it out of the house — once someone else gets to experience it — everything is changed.

You are changed. The project is changed. The audience is changed.

That's the alchemy of art.

Here's a real-life example. Nedi Safa, one of my clients, worked with her son to compose a song about autism. She finally got the courage to get it mastered, and she posted it online. She started getting emails and responses — including one from Kate Winslet's Golden Hat Foundation (www.goldenhatfoundation.org), and then she created a successful fund-raising campaign with Kickstarter to move the project into its next phase.

Inspiring, right?

Those critical voices will always be with you. It's up to you to decide if they get to run the show.

I can't guarantee you that getting your work out there will always lead to success. I *can* guarantee you that not getting your work out there will always lead to feelings of failure. Please let me know how it goes for you.

Remember: *The world needs your art.*

Acknowledgments

My heartfelt thanks go to:

My sisters: Andrea Goetz and Laura Bennett

My parents: Beatrice B. Briggs, Gunnar Bennett, and Kay Banks

My heart: Sasha and Foster

My husbands: Ron West and Stephen Ramsey

My mostly husband: Luke Hannington

My north star: Amy Ahlers

My whole crew: Margaret Weber, Tish Hicks, Sarah Sullivan, Dara Carr, Kate Taylor

My education: the Second City, the Open Fist Theatre Company, ComedySportz, LA Theatre Works, Sam Christensen Studios, Larry Levinson Productions, and all those other half-time, part-time, sometimes, and all-the-time gigs that helped me keep body and soul together.

My celebrity boyfriend: Ed O'Neill

My without-your-critical-support-this-book-wouldn't-exist folks: Dyana Valentine, Betsy Amster, Phillip Goetz, Lisa Elia

My teachers: Sam Christensen, David Neagle, Elisabeth Manning, Rev. William Thomas Jr., Rev. Michael Kosik, Phil Swann, Amanda Swann, Steph Tuss, and Mary Dombrowski

My TOAC family: Leonore Tjia, LongerDays.com, the Get It Done alumni, the 365 Club, the Creative Genius CEOs, and my VIP private clients

My grandmothers: Daga Ramsey and Virginia Briggs

My Girl Genius Small Business Success Club: Shannan Vergow, Melissa McFarlane, Jennifer Hardaway, Georgia Reed, Stephanie Miller, Laura Hall, Kara Ortiz, Katy Tafoya, and James Hallett, honorary girl

My small-business marketing gurus: all my Infusionsoft pals

My New World Library Council of Geniuses: Georgia Hughes, Mimi Kusch, Kristen Cashman, Jonathan Wichmann, Tona Pearce Myers, and Monique Muhlenkamp.

Endnotes

Chapter Three: Your Creativity Toolkit

Page 34 *It's called* acedia: According to Answers.com and Encyclopedia Brittanica.com, respectively.

Page 35 *As Tony Hsieh, author of* Delivering Happiness: Tony Hsieh, *Delivering Happiness: A Path to Profits, Passion, and Purpose* (New York: Hachette, 2010), 232.

Page 39 *students of the arts in all disciplines:* "Make Art. Save Art. Why Save Art?" DoSomething.org, undated, www.dosomething.org/make-art -save-art/why.

Chapter Four: Overcoming Perfectionism

Page 46 *There is a dark time in WordPress:* Matt Mullenweg, "1.0 Is the Loneliest Number," *Ma.tt: Unlucky in Cards* blog, November 9, 2010, Ma.tt/2010/11/one-point-oh. Mullenweg is one of *PC World*'s Top 50 People on the Web, *Inc.com*'s 30 under 30, *Business Week*'s 25 Most Influential People on the Web, and *Vanity Fair*'s Next Establishment.

Chapter Seven: Who Are You to Do This, Anyway?

Page 87 *"The inability to correctly perceive reality..."*: Tom Robbins, *Skinny Legs and All* (New York: Bantam, 1990), 64.

Page 91 *They were able to describe one another:* Much of the material in this chapter (and indeed, much of this book) was developed while

I was co-teaching with the brilliant Sam Christensen (www.Sam Christensen.com), who's been preaching about descriptive precision at his studio in Los Angeles and around the world for decades.

Chapter Fourteen: Beginning to Get Your Work Out There

Page 186 *Seven Easy Steps to Making a Profit* — *Today:* This seven-step process was originally created for the Get Your Work Out There VIP Program led by Steve Harper and me in June 2011.

Index

About the Author

Sam Bennett is the creator of the Organized Artist Company (www .TheOrganizedArtistCompany.com), dedicated to helping creative people get unstuck, especially by helping them focus and move forward on their goals.

Originally from Chicago and now living in a tiny, old-fashioned beach town outside Los Angeles, Samantha offers her revolutionary "Get It Done," "Get Your Work Out There," and "Creative Genius, CEO" workshops, teleclasses, public speaking engagements, and private consulting to overwhelmed procrastinators, frustrated overachievers, and recovering perfectionists everywhere.